ESSENTIAL POEMS
FOR BRITAIN

ESSENTIAL POEMS FOR BRITAIN

(and the way we live now)

EDITED BY

DAISY GOODWIN

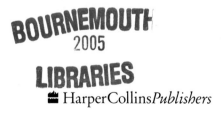
HarperCollins*Publishers*

For Teddy Lymans

HarperCollins*Publishers*
77–85 Fulham Palace Road,
Hammersmith, London W6 8JB

www.harpercollins.co.uk

By arrangement with the BBC
BBC © BBC 1996
The BBC logo is a registered trademark of
the British Broadcasting Corporation and
is used under licence.

Published by HarperCollins*Publishers* 2003
9 8 7 6 5 4 3 2 1

Full permissions information may be found on pp. 183–185

A catalogue record for this book
is available from the British Library

ISBN 0 00 716028 3

Set in PostScript Linotype Minion with Optima display
Typeset by Rowland Phototypesetting Ltd, Bury St Edmunds, Suffolk

CONTENTS

INTRODUCTION

As the editor of five anthologies that aim to prove that poetry is the ultimate in self help, it felt quite strange to be collecting poems about a place rather than a state of mind. Strange, that is, until I realized that, of course, being British IS a state of mind. Other countries besides ourselves have unpredictable weather, incomprehensible national sports, well tended gardens and neglected emotions, but no other nation regards them fondly as distinguishing characteristics. Surely no other member of the United Nations so well understands the zen of queuing, or that the pleasures of the flesh pale against the splendours of properly managed compost, or the art of the aggressive apology. Other countries have national days, we have garden centres and we're proud of them.

In compiling this book I have tried to strike a balance between poems that somehow affirm our sense of being British and those that aim to mock, deride or even console us for our heritage. Of course, because this is a British anthology consisting of British poets there was no shortage of poems that find fault with this country. I had to go back to an era when the map was still liberally daubed with pink to find poems that were unabashedly patriotic. Still I was relieved to find so many poems that poke fun at our national institutions: the monarchy, the weather, British rail, bad sex, rotten teeth. A nation that can laugh at itself so thoroughly is one to which I for one am proud to belong.

I should note here that I have not included separate categories for Wales, Scotland and Northern Ireland, although I have included poems by Welsh, Scottish and Northern Irish poets. I felt that the climate, a weakness for animals and gardens and execrable public transport were national afflictions and needed no further sub-division. The only exception to this is the collection of poems under the title 'Mad Dogs and Englishmen' but as these poems feature English bloodymindedness, I trust that Welsh, Scottish and Northern Irish readers won't object too much at being left out.

The subtitle for this book is *and the way we live now*. Some of the poems collected here are classics but many of them have been written comparatively recently. I wanted a book that could stretch from the nineteenth century patriotic certainties of Sir Walter Scott to the modern ambiguities of Jackie Kay's 'In My Country'. So, while there is a splendidly verdant section celebrating the glories of the countryside, there are poems about litter-strewn inner cities and coming off designer drugs. There are a clutch of poems that delineate a particularly British kind of loving: the world of *Brief Encounter* and things not said; but I have also included a quiver of poems, including some fine limericks, that show that we British enjoy smut as much as the next nation. There are poems about the glories of sport, poems written to console the long suffering partners of sportsmen and there are poems old and new about the miseries of the weather. British poets are consistent through the ages about few things, but in the course of my extensive research I don't think I came across one derogatory poem about a pet or a positive one about a journalist.

The most recent poems in the book are those shortlisted for the Poem For Britain competition which the BBC ran to celebrate

National Poetry Day. Viewers were invited to write a poem of no more than sixteen lines on the subject of Britain. There were over five thousand entries, many of them of such high quality that the judges Nigel Williams, Roger McGough and Caroline Gascgoine, the literary editor of the *Sunday Times*, had real difficulty in selecting the shortlist. What is interesting is that the winning poems, though very different in tone, share a perception of Britain as a country that, as they say in PowerPoint land, is struggling to find its core brand-values. Rule Britannia and Cool Britannia are both equally redundant: what these amateur poets found to celebrate was our lack of pretension, our pleasant shabbiness, our ability to compromise. The British reflected in these poems are past the first flush of youth, bulging here and there, wrongheaded on occasion but on the whole humane. One particular poem in the top three, 'Harvest Time', is stirring in its very lack of bravado. It seems somehow ultimately British that its author should be a management consultant, there is long tradition of besuited professions harbouring great poetry here: Larkin in his library, T.S. Eliot and Roy Fuller in their respective banks, even Robbie Burns was an Excise officer. Once upon a time there were even politician poets: the great metaphysical poet Andrew Marvell was the MP for Hull. Today I very much doubt whether any member of parliament would consider poetry an electoral asset.

As with my previous anthologies, I recommend taking this book slowly. You don't need much time to read any of the poems in this book but you do need to give them your full attention. Reading great poetry is like drinking serious wine, you don't gulp Château Margaux, you savour every costly molecule. Every word in a poem deserves the same respect. Of course, if having once really tasted a poem you still don't like it, move on. I hope there will be poems here for every taste. Use this book as a consolation when the-village-hall-if-wet-option becomes a sodden reality. Keep it with you when travelling round the country to remind yourself of those poetic landmarks like Adlestrop or Beeny Cliff or more prosaically to get you through the inevitable traffic jams and train cancellations. Have it to hand when visiting Post Offices, A&E departments, the January Sales or EuroDisney, the section on 'The Queue' is designed for just these situations. And refer to the 'Home Thoughts From Abroad' section when tempted by the thought of a life spent among olive groves: if the poets there are anything to go by, you will miss this country with all its limitations more than you could possibly imagine.

I could not have put this book together without Ned Williams, whose taste in poetry, though wildly different from mine, is impeccable. I am grateful to Jane Root, the controller of BBC2, for suggesting the theme of this book and the TV programme that accompanies it – compiling this book has made me realize how poetry is deeply embedded in our national psyche. Thanks too, to the judges of the Poem for Britain competition and to all the thousands of people who entered – the quality and range of the work submitted was outstanding. The best way to write poetry is to read it and I hope this book will prove a starting point for would-be poets everywhere.

ESSENTIAL POEMS FOR BRITAIN

A GREEN AND PLEASANT LAND

The seventeenth-century poet Andrew Marvell writes in his lush celebration of cultivated nature 'The Garden' that

> No white nor red was ever seen
> So amorous as this lovely green.

Many of the most famous poems in English celebrate the glories of nature. Poem after poem takes up the idea of a green (or in Wordsworth's case yellow) refuge from the miseries of daily life. Some of the poems here are glisteningly sensual – Keats writes of the swelling gourds of Autumn, Sylvia Plath about blackberries 'fat/with blue-red juices'. Some of the poems are poignant snapshots of a perfect moment: like the summer stillness interrupted only by bird-song in Edward Thomas' 'Adlestrop' – a moment which stands in stark contrast to the mud and sounds of gunfire that surrounded the poet in his World War One trench. But all the poems here celebrate the power of nature to remind us that there is a bigger picture, and that we are only passing through. And even when the last blade of grass is stifled by concrete, these poems will still shimmer. No one can tarmac over what Wordsworth calls 'the inward eye'.

Adlestrop

Yes, I remember Adlestrop –
The name, because one afternoon
Of heat the express-train drew up there
Unwontedly. It was late June.

The steam hissed. Someone cleared his throat.
No one left and no one came
On the bare platform. What I saw
Was Adlestrop – only the name

And willows, willow-herb, and grass,
And meadowsweet, and haycocks dry,
No whit less still and lonely fair
Than the high cloudlets in the sky.

And for that minute a blackbird sang
Close by, and round him, mistier,
Farther and farther, all the birds
Of Oxfordshire and Gloucestershire.

Edward Thomas

The Darkling Thrush

I leant upon a coppice gate
    When Frost was spectre-gray,
And Winter's dregs made desolate
    The weakening eye of day.
The tangled bine-stems scored the sky
    Like strings of broken lyres,
And all mankind that haunted nigh
    Had sought their household fires.

The land's sharp features seemed to be
    The Century's corpse outleant,
His crypt the cloudy canopy,
    The wind his death-lament.
The ancient pulse of germ and birth
    Was shrunken hard and dry,
And every spirit upon earth
    Seemed fervourless as I.

At once a voice arose among
    The bleak twigs overhead
In a full-hearted evensong
    Of joy illimited;
An aged thrush, frail, gaunt, and small,
    In blast-beruffled plume,
Had chosen thus to fling his soul
    Upon the growing gloom.

So little cause for carolings
    Of such ecstatic sound
Was written on terrestrial things
    Afar or nigh around,
That I could think there trembled through
    His happy good-night air
Some blessed Hope, whereof he knew
    And I was unaware.

Thomas Hardy

'I wandered lonely as a cloud'

I wandered lonely as a cloud
That floats on high o'er vales and hills,
When all at once I saw a crowd,
A host, of golden daffodils;
Beside the lake, beneath the trees,
Fluttering and dancing in the breeze.

Continuous as the stars that shine
And twinkle on the milky way,
They stretched in never-ending line
Along the margin of a bay:
Ten thousand saw I at a glance,
Tossing their heads in sprightly dance.

The waves beside them danced; but they
Out-did the sparkling waves in glee:
A poet could not but be gay,
In such a jocund company:
I gazed – and gazed – but little thought
What wealth the show to me had brought.

For oft, when on my couch I lie
In vacant or in pensive mood,
They flash upon that inward eye
Which is the bliss of solitude;
And then my heart with pleasure fills,
And dances with the daffodils.

William Wordsworth

The Way Through The Woods

They shut the road through the woods
Seventy years ago.
Weather and rain have undone it again,
And now you would never know
There was once a road through the woods
Before they planted the trees.
It is underneath the coppice and heath
And the thin anemones.
Only the keeper sees
That, where the ring-dove broods,
And the badgers roll at ease,
There was once a road through the woods.

Yet, if you enter the woods
Of a summer evening late,
When the night-air cools on the trout-ringed pools
Where the otter whistles his mate,
(They fear not men in the woods,
Because they see so few.)
You will hear the beat of a horse's feet,
And the swish of a skirt in the dew,
Steadily cantering through
The misty solitudes,
As though they perfectly knew
The old lost road through the woods . . . .
But there is no road through the woods.

Rudyard Kipling

To Autumn

Season of mists and mellow fruitfulness!
  Close bosom-friend of the maturing sun;
Conspiring with him how to load and bless
  With fruit the vines that round the thatch-eves run;
To bend with apples the moss'd cottage-trees,
  And fill all fruit with ripeness to the core;
    To swell the gourd, and plump the hazel shells
  With a sweet kernel; to set budding more,
And still more, later flowers for the bees,
Until they think warm days will never cease,
    For Summer has o'er-brimm'd their clammy cells.

Who hath not seen thee oft amid thy store?
  Sometimes whoever seeks abroad may find
Thee sitting careless on a granary floor,
  Thy hair soft-lifted by the winnowing wind;
Or on a half-reap'd furrow sound asleep,
  Drowsed with the fumes of poppies, while thy hook
    Spares the next swath and all its twined flowers:
And sometime like a gleaner thou dost keep
  Steady thy laden head across a brook;
  Or by a cyder-press, with patient look,
    Thou watchest the last oozings hours by hours.

Where are the songs of Spring? Ay, where are they?
    Think not of them, thou hast thy music too, –
While barred clouds bloom the soft-dying day,
    And touch the stubble-plains with rosy hue;
Then in a wailful choir the small gnats mourn
        Among the river sallows, borne aloft
            Or sinking as the light wind lives or dies;
And full-grown lambs loud bleat from hilly bourn;
        Hedge-crickets sing; and now with treble soft
        The red-breast whistles from a garden-croft;
            And gathering swallows twitter in the skies.

John Keats

Blackberrying

Nobody in the lane, and nothing, nothing but blackberries,
Blackberries on either side, though on the right mainly,
A blackberry alley, going down in hooks, and a sea
Somewhere at the end of it, heaving. Blackberries
Big as the ball of my thumb, and dumb as eyes
Ebon in the hedges, fat
With blue-red juices. These they squander on my fingers.
I had not asked for such a blood sisterhood; they must love me.
They accommodate themselves to my milkbottle, flattening
    their sides.

Overhead go the choughs in black, cacophonous flocks –
Bits of burnt paper wheeling in a blown sky.
Theirs is the only voice, protesting, protesting.
I do not think the sea will appear at all.
The high, green meadows are glowing, as if lit from within.
I come to one bush of berries so ripe it is a bush of flies,
Hanging their bluegreen bellies and their wing panes in a
    Chinese screen.
The honey-feast of the berries has stunned them; they believe
    in heaven.
One more hook, and the berries and bushes end.

The only thing to come now is the sea.
From between two hills a sudden wind funnels at me,
Slapping its phantom laundry in my face.
These hills are too green and sweet to have tasted salt.
I follow the sheep path between them. A last hook brings me
To the hills' northern face, and the face is orange rock
That looks out on nothing, nothing but a great space
Of white and pewter lights, and a din like silversmiths
Beating and beating at an intractable metal.

Sylvia Plath

Loveliest of Trees

Loveliest of trees, the cherry now
Is hung with bloom along the bough,
And stands about the woodland ride
Wearing white for Eastertide.

Now, of my threescore years and ten.
Twenty will not come again,
And take from seventy springs a score,
It only leaves me fifty more.

And since to look at things in bloom
Fifty springs are little room,
About the woodlands I will go
To see the cherry hung with snow.

A. E. Housman

My Garden

A garden is a lovesome thing, God wot!
Rose plot,
Fringed pool,
Ferned grot –
The veriest school
Of peace; and yet the fool
Contends that God is not –
Not God! in gardens! when the eve is cool?
Nay, but I have a sign;
'Tis very sure God walks in mine.

Thomas Edward Brown

from *The Garden*

What wondrous life is this I lead!
Ripe apples drop about my head;
The luscious clusters of the vine
Upon my mouth do crush their wine;
The nectarine, and curious peach,
Into my hands themselves do reach;
Stumbling on melons, as I pass,
Insnared with flowers, I fall on grass.

Meanwhile the mind, from pleasure less,
Withdraws into its happiness;
The mind, that ocean where each kind
Does straight its own resemblance find;
Yet it creates, transcending these,
Far other worlds, and other seas,
Annihilating all that's made
To a green thought in a green shade.

Andrew Marvell

LOVE IN A COLD CLIMATE

It seems to me quite British that the love poems here are as tight and suppressed as the poems about greenery in the previous section are warm and sensual. Perhaps a nation can't do both: the French have made sensuality an art but their gardens – full of gravel and clipped box hedges – are as restrained as Betjeman's unlikely lovers holding hands 'In A Bath Teashop'. U. A. Fanthorpe's 'Atlas' seemed to me a particularly British love poem. I can't imagine a poet from any other nation would cite the possession and proper usage of WD40 as proof of undying affection.

In 'An Arundel Tomb' Philip Larkin hedges his bets in language as sculpted as the effigy he is describing: the long forgotten Earl and Countess' clasped hands have come

To prove
Our almost instinct almost true:
What will survive of us is love.

This Englishwoman

This Englishwoman is so refined
She has no bosom and no behind.

Stevie Smith

The Civil Lovers

An after-kiss, it's kind of formal,
Like saying thank you for a supper.
Odd the thresholds we retreat from,
Uttering cries and all the normal
Decencies we've been brought up on.
After our feast of skin and fur
(Its carnal anger and its screaming),
We think such ritual blessings proper.

Many the couples who lie dreaming
In a coldly separate stillness
Of a talkative forgiveness
And a love that cannot weep.
But after knowledge comes a dull
Politeness and the wish to sleep.

Tom Paulin

Oxford

Oddbins, which I think opened when we were first married
   is packed. A pub we met for lunch in, the day
Dylan released *Street-Legal*, has changed name: town not gown,
   So I go to another and sit an hour with
ghosts and a pint. Recalling happiness a thwart thing
   killed hurts me worse than thoughts of the misery
we came to. Sites of memory. The winged years. If this
   is doing work on myself, I don't know, but when
I pass a shop and remember a dress, suddenly,
   after everything, there are tears on my cheek.

Lachlan MacKinnon

Atlas

There is a kind of love called maintenance,
Which stores the WD40 and knows when to use it;

Which checks the insurance, and doesn't forget
The milkman; which remembers to plant bulbs;

Which answers letters; which knows the way
The money goes; which deals with dentists

And Road Fund Tax and meeting trains,
And postcards to the lonely; which upholds

The permanently ricketty elaborate
Structures of living; which is Atlas.

And maintenance is the sensible side of love,
Which knows what time and weather are doing
To my brickwork; insulates my faulty wiring;
Laughs at my dryrotten jokes; remembers
My need for gloss and grouting; which keeps
My suspect edifice upright in air,
As Atlas did the sky.

U. A. Fanthorpe

40–Love

Middle	aged
couple	playing
ten	nis
when	the
game	ends
and	they
go	home
the	net
will	still
be	be
tween	them

Roger McGough

In a Bath Teashop

'Let us not speak, for the love we bear one another –
    Let us hold hands and look.'
She, such a very ordinary little woman;
    He, such a thumping crook;
But both, for a moment, little lower than the angels
    In the teashop's ingle-nook.

Sir John Betjeman

An Arundel Tomb

Side by side, their faces blurred,
The earl and countess lie in stone,
Their proper habits vaguely shown
As jointed armour, stiffened pleat,
And that faint hint of the absurd –
The little dogs under their feet.

Such plainness of the pre-baroque
Hardly involves the eye, until
It meets his left-hand gauntlet, still
Clasped empty in the other; and
One sees, with a sharp tender shock,
His hand withdrawn, holding her hand.

They would not think to lie so long.
Such faithfulness in effigy
Was just a detail friends would see:
A sculptor's sweet commissioned grace
Thrown off in helping to prolong
The Latin names around the base.

They would not guess how early in
Their supine stationary voyage
The air would change to soundless damage,
Turn the old tenantry away;
How soon succeeding eyes begin
To look, not read. Rigidly they

Persisted, linked, through lengths and breadths
Of time. Snow fell, undated. Light
Each summer thronged the glass. A bright
Litter of birdcalls strewed the same
Bone-riddled ground. And up the paths
The endless altered people came,

Washing at their identity.
Now, helpless in the hollow of
An unarmorial age, a trough
Of smoke in slow suspended skeins
Above their scrap of history,
Only an attitude remains:

Time has transfigured them into
Untruth. The stone fidelity
They hardly meant has come to be
Their final blazon, and to prove
Our almost-instinct almost true:
What will survive of us is love.

Philip Larkin

FOOD, GLORIOUS FOOD

These poems predate Delia, Nigella and Jamie and the final drizzle of virgin olive oil; the poets here are smacking their lips over the kind of robust fare – roast beef, grilled halibut, fresh shrimps – that needs no fancy presentation. Try Sydney Smith's recipe for a salad if you are worried about your cholesterol levels – I have and it is everything he claims!

The Roast Beef of Old England

When mighty roast Beef was the *Englishman's* Food,
It ennobled our Hearts, and enriched our Blood;
Our Soldiers were brave, and our Courtiers were good.
    Oh the Roast Beef of Old *England*,
    And Old *England's* Roast Beef!

Then, *Britons*, from all nice Dainties refrain,
Which effeminate *Italy, France*, and *Spain*;
And mighty Roast Beef shall command on the Main.
    Oh the Roast Beef, &c.

Henry Fielding

To the Immortal Memory of the Halibut

On which I dined this day,
Monday, April 26, 1784

Where hast thou floated, in what seas pursued
Thy pastime? when wast thou an egg new spawn'd,
Lost in th'immensity of ocean's waste?
Roar as they might, the overbearing winds
That rock'd the deep, thy cradle, thou wast safe–
And in thy minikin and embryo state,
Attach'd to the firm leaf of some salt weed,
Didst outlive tempests, such as wrung and rack'd
The joints of many a stout and gallant bark,
And whelm'd them in the unexplored abyss.
Indebted to no magnet and no chart,
Nor under guidance of the polar fire,
Thou wast a voyager on many coasts,
Grazing at large in meadows submarine,
Where flat Batavia, just emerging, peeps
Above the brine – where Caledonia's rocks
Beat back the surge – and where Hibernia shoots
Her wondrous causeway far into the main.
– Wherever thou hast fed, thou little thought'st,
And I not more, that I should feed on thee.

Peace, therefore, and good health, and much good fish
To him who sent thee! and success, as oft
As it descends into the billowy gulf,
To the same drag that caught thee! – Fare thee well!
Thy lot thy brethren of the slimy fin
Would envy, could they know that thou wast doom'd
To feed a bard, and to be praised in verse.

William Cowper

I'm a Shrimp! I'm a Shrimp!

I'm a shrimp! I'm a shrimp! Of diminutive size.
Inspect my antennae, and look at my eyes;
I'm a natural syphon, when dipped in a cup,
For I drain the contents to the latest drop up.
I care not for craw-fish, I heed not the prawn,
From a flavour especial my fame has been drawn;
Nor e'en to the crab or the lobster do yield,
When I'm properly cook'd and efficiently peeled.
Quick! Quick! pile the coals – let your saucepan be deep,
For the weather is warm, and I'm sure not to keep;
Off, off with my head – split my shell into three –
I'm a shrimp! I'm a shrimp – to be eaten with tea.

Robert Brough

A Little Lamb

Mary had a little lamb,
She ate it with mint sauce,
And everywhere that Mary went
The lamb went too, of course.

Anonymous

A Vegetation to Be Read by the Parsnip

Aubergine aubergine
Lettuce pray for the marrow
For no one radishes the end
We have all cucumbered our unworthy chives
With foul swedes
It ill beetroots us to publicly sprout pea
From the endive our fennels
None escapes the cabbages of thyme
Even the wisest sage comes to a spinach
Celery celery I say unto you
This is the cauliflower
When salsifiers all
Artichoke and kale.

B. C. Leale

Recipe for a Salad

To make this condiment, your poet begs
The pounded yellow of two hard-boiled eggs;
Two boiled potatoes, passed through kitchen-sieve,
Smoothness and softness to the salad give;
Let onion atoms lurk within the bowl,
And, half-suspected, animate the whole.
Of mordant mustard add a single spoon,
Distrust the condiment that bites so soon;
But deem it not, thou man of herbs, a fault,
To add a double quantity of salt.
And, lastly, o'er the flavored compound toss
A magic soup-spoon of anchovy sauce.
Oh, green and glorious! Oh, herbaceous treat!
'T would tempt the dying anchorite to eat;
Back to the world he'd turn his fleeting soul,
And plunge his fingers in the salad bowl!
Serenely full, the epicure would say,
Fate can not harm me, I have dined to-day!

Sydney Smith

THE SPORTING LIFE

There are some superb poems about sport by British poets.
I know nothing and want to know even less about cricket
or golf, but reading 'The Catch' by Simon Armitage and
'Seaside Golf' by John Betjeman has made even me
understand the immense satisfaction they have to offer.
I include 'Cricket Widow' and 'The Perfect Match' for the
long-suffering partners of sportsmen – and 'Not Cricket'
for a surprising and uncomfortable take on John Major's
favourite game.

The Catch

Forget
the long, smouldering
afternoon. It is

this moment
when the ball scoots
off the edge

of the bat; upwards,
backwards, falling
seemingly

beyond him
yet he reaches
and picks it

out
of its loop
like

an apple
from a branch,
the first of the season.

Simon Armitage

Seaside Golf

How straight it flew, how long it flew,
    It clear'd the rutty track
And soaring, disappeared from view
    Beyond the bunker's back –
A glorious, sailing, bounding drive
That made me glad I was alive.

And down the fairway, far along
    It glowed a lonely white;
I played an iron sure and strong
    And clipp'd it out of sight,
And spite of grassy banks between
I knew I'd find it on the green.

And so I did. It lay content
    Two paces from the pin;
A steady putt and then it went
    Oh, most securely in.
The very turf rejoiced to see
That quite unprecedented three.

Ah! seaweed smells from sandy caves
    And thyme and mist in whiffs,
In-coming tide, Atlantic waves
    Slapping the sunny cliffs,
Lark song and sea sounds in the air
And splendour, splendour everywhere.

Sir John Betjeman

Cricket Widow

Out of the love you bear me,
    By all its sweet beginnings,
Darling heart, please spare me
    The details of your innings.

Kit Wright

The Perfect Match

There is nothing like the five minutes to go:
Your lads one up, your lads one down, or the whole
    Thing even. How you actually feel,
        What you truly know,
Is that your lads are going to do it. So,

However many times in the past the fact
Is that they didn't, however you screamed and strained,
    Pummelled the floor, looked up and groaned
        As the Seiko ticked
On, when the ultimate ball is nodded or kicked.

The man in the air is you. Your beautiful wife
May curl in the corner yawningly calm and true,
    But something's going on with you
        That lasts male life.
Love's one thing, but this is the Big Chief.

Glyn Maxwell

Not Cricket

The television shows crowds of Indians
throwing things at men dressed in white.
Sky sports it says in the corner
and it looks hot and sticky.

Here it is wet outside and I
am just wetting my insides
with the first pint of the day.
No one is watching this new sport
of throwing things at men dressed in white
but myself, I suppose they have
seen it all before, though it does
look an unequal contest to me.

I suppose I will begin to see
the point of it all after
my second pint, and of course
I do. The unequal contest we like
to call life seems winnable once again
and I sit up straight and begin
to root for the Indians, who need
no help from me at all.

Go get them I say loudly
kill the sods I say. One of the men
in white is hit on the head
by something and I cheer
supposing this to be the object
of the game. I lean forward
and ask the barman who's winning
and puzzlingly he points to the door.

Henry Graham

QUEEN AND COUNTRY

It is impossible to compile an anthology about Britain
today without some reference to royalty. Oddly enough,
none of the poems I have chosen are by Poet Laureates
whose job it is to give the monarchy the requisite poetic
spin. I've gone for rather less reverent verse, like the
sprightly poem by Sophie Hannah about the marriage
of Edward and Sophie, which was commissioned by the
Daily Mail but never printed. I wonder why.

Impromptu on Charles II

God bless our good and gracious King,
Whose promise none relies on;
Who never said a foolish thing,
Nor ever did a wise one.

John Wilmot, Second Earl of Rochester

On Proposed Legislation to Prevent British Women Importing Foreign Husbands

A thing of which we do not speak –
the Queen is married to a Greek!

Gavin Ewart

Buckingham Palace

They're changing guard at Buckingham Palace –
Christopher Robin went down with Alice.
Alice is marrying one of the guard.
'A soldier's life is terrible hard,'
                                        Says Alice.

They're changing guard at Buckingham Palace –
Christopher Robin went down with Alice.
We saw a guard in a sentry-box.
'One of the sergeants looks after their socks,'
                                        Says Alice.

They're changing guard at Buckingham Palace –
Christopher Robin went down with Alice.
We looked for the King, but he never came.
'Well, God take care of him, all the same,'
                                        Says Alice.

They're changing guard at Buckingham Palace –
Christopher Robin went down with Alice.
They've great big parties inside the grounds.
'I wouldn't be King for a hundred pounds,'
                                        Says Alice.

They're changing guard at Buckingham Palace –
Christopher Robin went down with Alice.
A face looked out, but it wasn't the King's.
'He's much too busy a-signing things,'

Says Alice.

They're changing guard at Buckingham Palace –
Christopher Robin went down with Alice.
'Do you think the King knows all about *me*?'
'Sure to, dear, but it's time for tea,'

Says Alice.

A. A. Milne

Royal Wedding Poem

I have attended weddings in the past
Where I'm the only person in the room
To harbour an intransigent and vast
Landmass of spite towards the bride and groom.
I have attended weddings with my coat
Buttoned against the hot, ecstatic horde
Throughout the service, wearing a remote
Glaze to appear above it all and bored.

At last, a marriage I can celebrate:
No choruses of 'Oh, you have to come!'
No one I liked once but have grown to hate
But must make small-talk with to please my mum.
Weddings involving nobody one knows –
What a good plan. I'll vote for more of those.

Sophie Hannah

CATS AND DOGS

I am always being asked to recommend poems that mark
the passing of a beloved pet. This may be a minor rite of
passage but it affects people very deeply and poets are
no exception. 'Four feet' by Rudyard Kipling will be
appreciated by anyone who has lost a faithful companion.
I include a tart little poem 'O happy dogs of England' by
Stevie Smith to redress the balance slightly. How British
is it that we give so much more to the RSPCA than the
NSPCC?

O Happy Dogs of England

O happy dogs of England
Bark well as well you may
If you lived anywhere else
You would not be so gay.

Stevie Smith

For I Will Consider My Cat Jeoffry

For I will consider my cat Jeoffry
[. . .] For having done duty and received blessing he begins to
    consider himself.
For this he performs in ten degrees.
For first he looks upon his fore-paws to see if they are clean.
For secondly he kicks up behind to clear away there.

For thirdly he works it upon stretch with the fore paws extended.
For forthly he sharpens his paws by wood.
For fifthly he washes himself.
For sixthly he rolls upon wash.
For Seventhly he fleas himself, that he may not be interrupted
    upon the beat.
For Eighthly he rubs himself against a post.
For Ninthly he looks up for his instructions.
For Tenthly he goes in quest of food.
For having consider'd God and himself he will consider his
    neighbour.
For if he meets another cat he will kiss her in kindness.
For when he takes his prey he plays with it to give it chance.
For one mouse in seven escapes by his dallying.
For when his day's work is done his business more properly begins.
For keeps the Lord's watch in the night against the adversary.

For he counteracts the powers of darkness by his electrical skin &
   glaring eyes.
For he counteracts the Devil, who is death, by brisking about
   the life.
For in his morning orisons he loves the sun and the sun loves him.
For he is of the tribe of Tiger.

Christopher Smart

On a Favourite Cat Drowned
in a Tub of Goldfishes

'Twas on a lofty vase's side,
Where China's gayest art had dyed
    The azure flowers that blow;
Demurest of the tabby kind,
The pensive Selima reclined,
    Gazed on the lake below.

Her conscious tail her joy declared;
The fair round face, the snowy beard,
    The velvet of her paws,
Her coat, that with the tortoise vies,
Her ears of jet, and emerald eyes,
    She saw; and purr'd applause.

Still had she gazed; but 'midst the tide
Two angel forms were seen to glide,
    The Genii of the stream:
Their scaly armour's Tyrian hue
Thro' richest purple to the view
    Betray'd a golden gleam.

The hapless Nymph with wonder saw:
A whisker first and then a claw,
 With many an ardent wish,
She stretch'd in vain to reach the prize.
What female heart can gold despise?
 What Cat's averse to fish?

Presumptuous Maid! with looks intent
Again she stretch'd, again she bent,
 Nor knew the gulf between.
(Malignant Fate sat by, and smiled.)
The slipp'ry verge her feet beguiled,
 She tumbled headlong in.

Eight times emerging from the flood
She mew'd to ev'ry wat'ry god,
 Some speedy aid to send.
No Dolphin came, no Nereid stirr'd:
Nor cruel *Tom*, nor *Susan* heard.
 A Fav'rite has no friend!

From hence, ye Beauties undeceived,
Know, one false step is ne'er retrieved,
 And be with caution bold.
Not all that tempts your wand'ring eyes
And heedless hearts, is lawful prize;
 Nor all that glisters, gold.

Thomas Gray

Four-Feet

('*The Woman in his Life*')

I have done mostly what most men do,
And pushed it out of my mind;
But I can't forget, if I wanted to,
Four-Feet trotting behind.

Day after day, the whole day through –
Wherever my road inclined –
Four-Feet said, 'I am coming with you!'
And trotted along behind.

Now I must go by some other round, –
Which I shall never find –
Somewhere that does not carry the sound
Of Four-Feet trotting behind.

Rudyard Kipling

Burying Moses

Moses was very old,
Ninety-eight, my grandpa said,
So we shouldn't cry too much
Now poor old Moses was dead.

Moses used to be black
But he slowly turned grey as a fog,
And snuffled and wheezed and snored.
Moses was our old dog.

Each year that people live
Counts for a dog as seven.
'He was a good old boy,' said Grandpa,
'He's sure to go to heaven.

'But first we must go and bury him
At the back of the garden shed,
So come and give me a hand;
We'll make him a deep warm bed.'

And so we lowered old Moses
Down in the hole Grandpa dug,
And he huddled there in a bundle
Like a dusty old fireside rug.

Then we filled in the hole and patted
The soil down smooth and flat.
'I'll make him a cross,' said Grandpa.
'The least we can do is that.

'He'll be wagging his tail in heaven,
So you mustn't be too upset . . .'
But Grandpa's voice sounded croaky,
And I could see his old cheeks were wet.

Vernon Scannell

IN MY COUNTRY

I have taken the title of this section about what it is to be
British from Jackie Kay's powerful poem. Her parentage
is of mixed race but she was adopted as a baby by a white
couple and brought up in Glasgow. Her sense of belonging
is altogether more complex than the simple patriotic
certainties of Sir Walter Scott, but both poets know which
country they call home. I have included 'I remember,
I remember' by Philip Larkin for the sardonic way it
undermines the narrative conventions of small-town-boy-
makes-good. Larkin, one feels, doesn't belong anywhere.

In my country

walking by the waters
down where an honest river
shakes hands with the sea,
a woman passed round me
in a slow watchful circle,
as if I were a superstition;

or the worst dregs of her imagination,
so when she finally spoke
her words spliced into bars
of an old wheel. A segment of air.
Where do you come from?
'Here,' I said, 'Here. These parts.'

Jackie Kay

from *The Lay of the Last Minstrel*

Breathes there the man, with soul so dead,
Who never to himself hath said,
    This is my own, my native land!
Whose heart hath ne'er within him burn'd,
As home his footsteps he hath turn'd,
    From wandering on a foreign strand!
If such there breathe, go, mark him well;
For him no Minstrel raptures swell;
High though his titles, proud his name,
Boundless his wealth as wish can claim;
Despite those titles, power, and pelf,
The wretch, concentred all in self,
Living, shall forfeit fair renown,
And, doubly dying, shall go down
To the vile dust, from whence he sprung,
Unwept, unhonour'd, and unsung.

Sir Walter Scott

Arrival 1946

The boat docked in at Liverpool.
From the train Tariq stared
at an unbroken line of washing
from the North West to Euston.

These are strange people, he thought –
an Empire, and all this washing,
the underwear, the Englishman's garden.
It was Monday, and very sharp.

Moniza Alvi

I Remember, I Remember

Coming up England by a different line
For once, early in the cold new year,
We stopped, and, watching men with number-plates
Sprint down the platform to familiar gates,
'Why, Coventry!' I exclaimed. 'I was born here.'

I leant far out, and squinnied for a sign
That this was still the town that had been 'mine'
So long, but found I wasn't even clear
Which side was which. From where those cycle-crates
Were standing, had we annually departed

For all those family hols? . . . A whistle went:
Things moved. I sat back, staring at my boots.
'Was that,' my friend smiled, 'where you "have your roots"?'
No, only where my childhood was unspent,
I wanted to retort, just where I started:

By now I've got the whole place clearly charted.
Our garden, first: where I did not invent
Blinding theologies of flowers and fruits,
And wasn't spoken to by an old hat.
And here we have that splendid family

I never ran to when I got depressed,
The boys all biceps and the girls all chest,
Their comic Ford, their farm where I could be
'Really myself'. I'll show you, come to that,
The bracken where I never trembling sat,

Determined to go through with it; where she
Lay back, and 'all became a burning mist'.
And, in those offices, my doggerel
Was not set up in blunt ten-point, nor read
By a distinguished cousin of the mayor,

Who didn't call and tell my father *There
Before us, had we the gift to see ahead* –
'You look as if you wished the place in Hell,'
My friend said, 'judging from your face.' 'Oh well,
I suppose it's not the place's fault,' I said.

'Nothing, like something, happens anywhere.'

Philip Larkin

TOOTH AND NAIL

When I lived in New York in my early twenties, I could always spot a fellow Brit in a crowd on account of their teeth which, like mine, would be crooked and mottled. (Americans, of course, all have gleaming white, straight teeth.) But, at least, as these poems prove, we can laugh at the fact that we are, as a nation, dentally challenged.

Teeth

English Teeth, English Teeth!
Shining in the sun
A part of British heritage
Aye, each and every one.

English Teeth, Happy Teeth!
Always having fun
Clamping down on bits of fish
And sausages half done.

English Teeth! HEROES' Teeth!
Hear them click! and clack!
Let's sing a song of praise to them –
Three Cheers for the Brown Grey and Black.

Spike Milligan

Crown and Country

When you come to our country
you will realise we are big on dentistry:
at the border your mouth will be opened, flossed
and an elegant silver filling stamped into D10.
Then you will catch the hygienic autobus, *Tooth
Fairy Express* smiling the improved smile of our people

who all know dentures are more crucial
than culture. We do not talk much, we say
cheese; pints of creamy gleaming teeth,
pouring out our white grins, our gold caps; smirks.
Just across the border, people have hellish holes,
gaping gaps, rotten roots, abscesses.

We identify people by their bite.
The lower class have most unusual bites.
They are sick to the back teeth.
At 2 a.m. on a hot dusty night in out town
you will hear the fraught percussion
of the entire population grinding its teeth.

Our dentists are the richest in the world,
mining our gobs of gold. They love the old;
the ones who finally succumb to receding gums,
to teeth falling haplessly out like hailstones.
Be careful of the wind; it can make your mouth fly wide.
All along this natural canal, you will note,
our wild poppies pout; lush red lips.

Jackie Kay

Oh, I Wish I'd Looked after me Teeth

Oh, I wish I'd looked after me teeth,
   And spotted the perils beneath
All the toffees I chewed,
   And the sweet sticky food.
Oh, I wish I'd looked after me teeth.

I wish I'd been that much more willin'
   When I had more tooth there than fillin'
To give up gobstoppers,
   From respect to me choppers,
And to buy something else with me shillin'.

When I think of the lollies I licked
   And the liquorice allsorts I picked,
Sherbet dabs, big and little,
   All that hard peanut brittle,
My conscience gets horribly pricked.

My mother, she told me no end,
   'If you got a tooth, you got a friend.'
I was young then, and careless,
   My toothbrush was hairless,
I never had much time to spend.

Oh I showed them the toothpaste all right,
    I flashed it about late at night,
But up-and-down brushin'
    And pokin' and fussin'
Didn't seem worth the time – I could bite!

If I'd known I was paving the way
    To cavities, caps and decay,
The murder of fillin's,
    Injections and drillin's,
I'd have thrown all me sherbet away.

So I lay in the old dentist's chair,
    And I gaze up his nose in despair,
And his drill it do whine
    In these molars of mine.
'Two amalgam,' he'll say, 'for in there.'

How I laughed at my mother's false teeth,
    As they foamed in the waters beneath.
But now comes the reckonin'
    It's *me* they are beckonin'
Oh, I *wish* I'd looked after me teeth.

Pam Ayres

UPSTAIRS, DOWNSTAIRS

I hope that class distinctions, as revealed by the way
people speak, don't matter as much today as they did
when Betjeman wrote 'How to Get On in Society'.
(Although I did recently overhear a Mercedes-driving
mother say that she didn't mind the kids swearing, but
would disown them if they said 'toilet' instead of 'loo'.)
If you want an antidote to all the petty snobberies of
British life, read 'National Trust' by Tony Harrison.
It is a timely reminder of what lies beneath the
sanitized version of our history known as 'heritage'.

Lord Finchley

Lord Finchley tried to mend the Electric Light
Himself. It struck him dead: And serve him right!
It is the business of the wealthy man
To give employment to the artisan.

Hilaire Belloc

How to Get On in Society

Phone for the fish-knives, Norman
    As Cook is a little unnerved;
You kiddies have crumpled the serviettes
    And I must have things daintily served.

Are the requisites all in the toilet?
    The frills round the cutlets can wait
Till the girl has replenished the cruets
    And switched on the logs in the grate

It's ever so close in the lounge dear,
    But the vestibule's comfy for tea
And Howard is out riding on horseback
    So do come and take some with me.

Now here is a fork for your pastries
    And do use the couch for your feet;
I know what I wanted to ask you –
    Is trifle sufficient for sweet?

Milk and then just as it comes dear?
    I'm afraid the preserve's full of stones;
Beg pardon, I'm soiling the doileys
    With afternoon tea-cakes and scones.

Sir John Betjeman

The Justice of the Peace

Distinguish carefully between these two,
    This thing is yours, that other thing is mine.
You have a shirt, a brimless hat, a shoe
    And half a coat. I am the Lord benign
Of fifty hundred acres of fat land
To which I have a right. You understand?

I have a right because I have, because,
    Because I have – because I have a right.
Now be quite calm and good, obey the laws,
    Remember your low station, do not fight
Against the goad, because, you know, it pricks
Whenever the uncleanly demos kicks.

I do not envy you your hat, your shoe.
    Why should you envy me my small estate?
It's fearfully illogical in you
    To fight with economic force and fate.
Moreover, I have got the upper hand,
And mean to keep it. Do you understand?

Hilaire Belloc

National Trust

Bottomless pits. There's one in Castleton,
and stout upholders of our law and order
one day thought its depth worth wagering on
and borrowed a convict hush-hush from his warder
and winched him down; and back, flayed, grey, mad, dumb.

Not even a good flogging made him holler.

O gentlemen, a better way to plumb
the depths of Britain's dangling a scholar,
say, here at the booming shaft at Towanroath,
now National Trust, a place where they got tin,
those gentlemen who silenced the men's oath
and killed the language that they swore it in.

The dumb go down in history and disappear
and not one gentleman's been brought to book:

Mes den hep tavas a-gollas y dyr

(Cornish) – 'the tongueless man gets his land took.'

Tony Harrison

LEAVES ON THE LINE

Transport is a very British preoccupation. Any failure of public transport is, like the weather (of which more later), an irreproachable excuse.

'Why are you late?'

'The trains/bus/tube . . .'

'Oh.'

The poems in this section reflect in various ways the vagaries of getting around in this country. I know British Rail no longer exists, but I felt that the poem 'British Rail Regrets', was still, sadly, relevant. For a completely different slant on travel read G. K. Chesterton's splendid poem 'The Rolling English Road'.

A-Have-it-Away-Day

I asked a friend how I lost her
'She met a man on a train
                    and fell in love with him.'
Money is not all the British Railways are
                                    losing.

Spike Milligan

British Rail Regrets

British Rail regrets
having to regret.
British Rail regrets
it cannot spell.
British Rail regrets
the chalk ran out.
British Rail regrets
that due to a staff shortage
there will be no one
to offer regrets.
British Rail regrets
but will not be sending
flowers or tributes.
British Rail regrets
the early arrival
of your train.
This was due to industrious action.
British Rail regrets
that because of a work-to-rule
by our tape machine
this is a real person.
British Rail regrets
the cheese shortage
in your sandwich.
This is due to
a points failure.

The steward got
three out of ten.
British Rail regrets.
Tears flow from beneath
the locked doors of the staff rooms.
red-eyed ticket collectors
offer comfort
to stranded passengers.
Angry drivers threaten
to come out in sympathy
with the public.
British Rail regrets.
That's why its members
are permanently dressed in black.
That's why porters stand around
as if in a state of shock.
That's why Passenger Information
is off the hook. British Rail regrets
that due to the shortage of regrets
there will be a train.

Steve Turner

Men on Trains 2

The big man who sits opposite
Is holding a mobile phone.
He dials a number carefully
And listens to it drone.

Someone answers and he says
Hallo hallo it's me.
His voice is oddly dangerous.
I pretend to drink cold tea.

I'm phoning from the hospital
He whines. (We shunt past Leeds).
The operation might not work
Or perhaps they can cure me.

Perhaps they can cure me,
He says, while nibbling a bit of cheese,
I just wish you'd phone me up
sometimes. Just once. Please.

Julia Darling

Toilet

I wonder will I speak to the girl
sitting opposite me on this train.
I wonder will my mouth open and say,
'Are you going all the way
to Newcastle?' or 'Can I get you a coffee?'
Or will it simply go 'aaaaah'
as if it had a mind of its own?

Half closing eggshell blue eyes,
she runs her hand through her hair
so that it clings to the carriage cloth,
then slowly frees itself.
She finds a brush and her long fair hair
flies back and forth like an African fly-whisk,
making me feel dizzy.

Suddenly, without warning,
she packs it all away in a rubber band
because I have forgotten to look out
the window for a moment.
A coffee is granted permission
to pass between her lips
and does so eagerly, without fuss.

A tunnel finds us looking out the window
into one another's eyes. She leaves her seat,
but I know that she likes me
because the light saying 'TOILET'
has come on, a sign that she is lifting
her skirt, taking down her pants
and peeing all over my face.

Hugo Williams

Waiting for the 242

There must be a better activity at a bus stop
    To which the mind can aspire
Than brooding upon the unnatural nature of nature
    And the undesirability of desire.

Kit Wright

The Rolling English Road

Before the Roman came to Rye or out to Severn strode,
The rolling English drunkard made the rolling English road.
A reeling road, a rolling road, that rambles round the shire,
And after him the parson ran, the sexton and the squire;
A merry road, a mazy road, and such as we did tread
The night we went to Birmingham by way of Beachy Head.

I knew no harm of Bonaparte and plenty of the Squire,
And for to fight the Frenchman I did not much desire;
But I did bash their baggonets because they came arrayed
To straighten out the crooked road an English drunkard made,
Where you and I went down the lane with ale-mugs in our hands,
The night we went to Glastonbury by way of Goodwin Sands.

His sins they were forgiven him: or why do flowers run
Behind him: and the hedges all strengthening in the sun?
The wild thing went from left to right and knew not which was
    which,
But the wild rose was above him when they found him in the ditch.
God pardon us, nor harden us; we did not see so clear
The night we went to Bannockburn by way of Brighton Pier.

My friends, we will not go again or ape an ancient rage
Or stretch the folly of our youth to be the shame of age,
But walk with clearer eyes and ears this path that wandereth,
And see undrugged in evening light the decent inn of death;
For there is good news yet to hear and fine things to be seen,
Before we go to Paradise by way of Kensal Green.

G. K. Chesterton

SHOWERS FORECAST

For some reason (sun spots possibly) this is the longest section in the book. The poems range from the comically bleak like 'English Weather' by Wendy Cope, to the straightforwardly bleak like 'Rain' by Edward Thomas. Does our weather affect our national character? The Caribbean poet Andrew Salkey has the answer in 'A Song For England'. But my favourite poem here has to be Seamus Heaney's marvellous poem about listening to the Shipping Forecast. It's even better than the real thing.

Rain

A million sardines
flapping insane on
the wet-velvet tarmac.

Des Dillon

English Weather

January's grey and slushy,
February's chill and drear,
March is wild and wet and windy,
April seldom brings much cheer.
In May, a day or two of sunshine,
Three or four in June, perhaps.
July is usually filthy,
August skies are open taps.
In September things start dying,
Then comes cold October mist.
November we make plans to spend
The best part of December pissed.

Wendy Cope

No!

No sun—no moon!
No morn—no noon—
No dawn—no dusk—no proper time of day—
   No sky—no earthly view—
   No distance looking blue—
No road—no street—no 't'other side the way'—
   No end to any Row—
   No indications where the Crescents go—
   No top to any steeple—
No recognitions of familiar people—
   No courtesies for showing 'em—
   No knowing 'em!—
No travelling at all—no locomotion,
No inkling of the way—no notion—
   'No go'—by land or ocean—
   No mail—no post—
No news from any foreign coast—
No Park—no Ring—no afternoon gentility—
   No company—no nobility—
No warmth, no cheerfulness, no healthful ease,
   No comfortable feel in any member—
No shade, no shine, no butterflies, no bees,
   No fruits, no flowers, no leaves, no birds,—
      November!

Thomas Hood

My Brollie

My grey suit matching English skies
I took a spiral stride
down the April pavements.

I had made a truce with rain
and almost felt Anglo-saxon
My at-homeness was heaven-sent.

A bobby doffed his helmet
in my foot-weaving direction
and the pigeons kept their distance.

All the signs told me to dance
or at least open my brollie
like some forgotten icon

So whether clouds play foul or fair
I wave my brollie's royal web
and embrace the anonymous air.

John Agard

from *Glanmore Sonnets*

Dogger, Rockall, Malin, Irish Sea:
Green, swift upsurges, North Atlantic flux
Conjured by that strong gale-warning voice,
Collapse into a sibilant penumbra.
Midnight and closedown. Sirens of the tundra,
Of eel-road, seal-road, keel-road, whale-road, raise
Their wind-compounded keen behind the baize
And drive the trawlers to the lee of Wicklow.
L'Etoile, Le Guillemot, La Belle Hélène
Nursed their bright names this morning in the bay
That toiled like mortar. It was marvellous
And actual, I said out loud, 'A haven,'
The word deepening, clearing, like the sky
Elsewhere on Minches, Cromarty, The Faroes

Seamus Heaney

Something Coming

The pavement shone with news of something coming,
or just with rain. She took it as a warning,
identical to last time – first the humming,
then thunder, then his letter in the morning.

She did her best to see some sort of sense
in all these things, to make them fit together.
At the same time she laughed at the pretence
that love could be connected with the weather,

which can't be true, or life would be too frightening
to live. Next time she swore she'd go to bed
and not stay up to study trends of lightning
and wonder what, if anything, they said.

Sophie Hannah

Henley Regatta

She looks from the window: still it pours down direly,
And the avenue drips. She cannot go, she fears;
And the Regatta will be spoilt entirely;
   And she sheds half-crazed tears.

Regatta Day and rain come on together
Again, years after. Gutters trickle loud;
But Nancy cares not. She knows nought of weather,
   Or of the Henley crowd:

She's a Regatta quite her own. Inanely
She laughs in the asylum as she floats
Within a water-tub, which she calls 'Henley',
   Her little paper boats.

Thomas Hardy

Rain

Rain, midnight rain, nothing but the wild rain
On this bleak hut, and solitude, and me
Remembering again that I shall die
And neither hear the rain nor give it thanks
For washing me cleaner than I have been
Since I was born into this solitude.
Blessed are the dead that the rain rains upon:
But here I pray that none whom once I loved
Is dying tonight or lying still awake
Solitary, listening to the rain,
Either in pain or thus in sympathy
Helpless among the living and the dead,
Like a cold water among broken reeds,
Myriads of broken reeds all still and stiff,
Like me who have no love which this wild rain
Has not dissolved except the love of death,
If love it be towards what is perfect and
Cannot, the tempest tells me, disappoint.

Edward Thomas

A Song for England

An' a so de rain a-fall
An' a so de snow a-rain

An' a so de fog a-fall
An' a so de sun a-fail

An' a so de seasons mix
An' a so de bag-o'-tricks

But a so me understan'
De misery o' de Englishman.

Andrew Salkey

FLYING THE FLAG

There is little doubt that lines from these poems: Kipling's 'If–', Blake's 'Jerusalem', and from Richard II are deeply embedded in the national consciousness. I remember weeping over Rupert Brooke's 'The Soldier' when I was eleven, and even today, although I have read more realistic World War One poems by the likes of Wilfred Owen, I am still stirred by 'The Soldier's' naïve glamour. The last poem in this section, 'Preparations', is a kind of counterweight to Kipling's 'If–'. Both celebrate a certain kind of stoicism which, I hope, is still a British thing.

from *Richard II, Act II*

This royal throne of kings, this sceptred isle,
This earth of majesty, this seat of Mars,
This other Eden, demi-paradise,
This fortress built by nature for herself
Against infection and the hand of war,
This happy breed of men, this little world,
This precious stone set in the silver sea,
Which serves it in the office of a wall,
Or as a moat defensive to a house
Against the envy of less happier lands;
This blessed plot, this earth, this realm, this England,

William Shakespeare

Jerusalem

And did those feet in ancient time
Walk upon England's mountains green?
And was the holy Lamb of God
On England's pleasant pastures seen?

And did the Countenance Divine
Shine forth upon our clouded hills?
And was Jerusalem builded here
Among these dark Satanic Mills?

Bring me my Bow of burning gold:
Bring me my Arrows of desire:
Bring me my Spear: O clouds unfold!
Bring me my Chariot of fire.

I will not cease from Mental Fight,
Nor shall my Sword sleep in my hand
Till we have built Jerusalem
In England's green & pleasant Land.

William Blake

If —

If you can keep your head when all about you
    Are losing theirs and blaming it on you,
If you can trust yourself when all men doubt you,
    But make allowance for their doubting too;
If you can wait and not be tired by waiting,
    Or being lied about, don't deal in lies,
Or being hated, don't give way to hating,
    And yet don't look too good, nor talk too wise:

If you can dream – and not make dreams your master;
    If you can think – and not make thoughts your aim;
If you can meet with Triumph and Disaster
    And treat those two impostors just the same;
If you can bear to hear the truth you've spoken
    Twisted by knaves to make a trap for fools,
Or watch the things you gave your life to, broken,
    And stoop and build 'em up with worn-out tools:

If you can make one heap of all your winnings
    And risk it on one turn of pitch-and-toss,
And lose, and start again at your beginnings
    And never breathe a word about your loss;
If you can force your heart and nerve and sinew
    To serve your turn long after they are gone,
And so hold on when there is nothing in you
    Except the Will which says to them: 'Hold on!'

If you can talk with crowds and keep your virtue,
    Or walk with Kings – nor lose the common touch,
If neither foes nor loving friends can hurt you,
    If all men count with you, but none too much;
If you can fill the unforgiving minute
    With sixty seconds' worth of distance run,
Yours is the Earth and everything that's in it,
    And – which is more – you'll be a Man, my son!

Rudyard Kipling

The Soldier

If I should die, think only this of me:
    That there's some corner of a foreign field
That is for ever England. There shall be
    In that rich earth a richer dust concealed;
A dust whom England bore, shaped, made aware,
    Gave, once, her flowers to love, her ways to roam,
A body of England's, breathing English air.
    Washed by the rivers, blest by suns of home.

And think, this heart, all evil shed away,
    A pulse in the eternal mind, no less
        Gives somewhere back the thoughts by England
           given;
Her sights and sounds; dreams happy as her day;
    And laughter, learnt of friends; and gentleness,
        In hearts at peace, under an English heaven.

Rupert Brooke

Preparations

In the valley there is an order to these things:
Chapel suits and the morning shift called off.
She takes the bus to Pontypridd to buy black,
But the men alone proceed to the grave,
Neighbours, his butties, and the funeral regulars.
The women are left in the house; they bustle
Around the widow with a hushed, furious
Energy that keeps grief out of the hour.
She holds to the kitchen, concerned with sandwiches.
It is a ham-bone big as a man's arm and the meat
Folds over richly from her knife. A daughter sits
Watching butter swim in its dish before the fire.
The best china laid precisely across the new tablecloth:
They wait. They count the places over and over like a rosary.

Tony Curtis

SEEN AND NOT HEARD

There are, of course, scores of poems about the wonders of a British childhood, but you won't find them here. The ones I have chosen are completely unsentimental in their take on what it is to be a child.

This lack of Disneyfication somehow seems to me more British.

Whole Duty of Children

A child should always say what's true,
And speak when he is spoken to,
And behave mannerly at table:
At least as far as he is able.

Robert Louis Stevenson

Henry King
who Chewed Bits of String,
and was Early Cut off
in Dreadful Agonies

The Chief Defect of Henry King
   Was chewing little bits of String.
At last he swallowed some which tied
   Itself in ugly Knots inside.
Physicians of the Utmost Fame
Were called at once; but when they came
They answered, as they took their Fees,
'There is no Cure for this Disease.
Henry will very soon be dead.'
His Parents stood about his Bed
Lamenting his Untimely Death,
When Henry, with his Latest Breath,
Cried – 'Oh, my Friends, be warned by me,
That Breakfast, Dinner, Lunch, and Tea
Are all the Human Frame requires . . .'
With that, the Wretched Child expires.

Hilaire Belloc

from *Alice in Wonderland*

Speak roughly to your little boy,
And beat him when he sneezes:
He only does it to annoy
Because he knows it teases.

Lewis Carroll

Timothy Winters

Timothy Winters comes to school
With eyes as wide as a football pool,
Ears like bombs and teeth like splinters:
A blitz of a boy is Timothy Winters.

His belly is white, his neck is dark,
And his hair is an exclamation mark.
His clothes are enough to scare a crow
And through his britches the blue winds blow.

When teacher talks he won't hear a word
And he shoots down dead the arithmetic-bird,
He licks the patterns off his plate
And he's not even heard of the Welfare State.

Timothy Winters has bloody feet
And he lives in a house on Suez Street,
He sleeps in a sack on the kitchen floor
And they say there aren't boys like him any more.

Old Man Winters likes his beer
And his missus ran off with a bombardier,
Grandma sits in the grate with a gin
And Timothy's dosed with an aspirin.

The Welfare Worker lies awake
But the law's as tricky as a ten-foot snake,
So Timothy Winters drinks his cup
And slowly goes on growing up.

At Morning Prayers the Master helves
For children less fortunate than ourselves,
And the loudest response in the room is when
Timothy Winters roars 'Ámen!'

So come one angel, come on ten:
Timothy Winters says 'Amen
Amen amen amen amen.'
Timothy Winters, Lord.
                                        Amen.

Charles Causley

CITY LIGHTS

The first two poems were written two hundred years apart but they share the same theme: that the pace of urban life is a drain on the spirit. 'Dunravin'' is an update of Byron's famous poem 'So We'll Go No More a Roving', which he wrote after a spectacular bout of debauchery at the Venice Carnival. The second two poems are about urban alienation, although written from very different perspectives.

'The world is too much with us; late and soon'

The world is too much with us; late and soon,
Getting and spending, we lay waste our powers:
Little we see in Nature that is ours;
We have given our hearts away, a sordid boon!
This Sea that bares her bosom to the moon;
And are up gathered now like sleeping flowers;
For this, for everything, we are out of tune;
It moves us not. – Great God! I'd rather be
A Pagan suckled in a creed outworn;
So might I, standing on this pleasant lea,
Have glimpses that would make me less forlorn;
Have sight of Proteus rising from the sea;
Or hear old Triton blow his wreathèd horn.

William Wordsworth

Dunravin'

(after Byron)

Though the tunes is just as bangin'
And the strobes is just as bright
We'll go no more a-ravin'
So late into the night

For my smile's become a rictus
My heart is pounding in my chest
It's 3am eternal
But I gotta get some rest

Though the night was made for ravin'
And the day returns too soon
Oh we'll go no more a-ravin'
By the light of the moon.

Tabitha Potts

London

I am the city of two divided cities
Where the eyes of rich and poor collide and wonder;
Where the beggar's voice is low and unexpectant,
And in clubs the feet of the servants are soft on the carpet
And the world's wind scarcely stirs the leaves of *The Times*.

I am the reticent, the private city,
The city of lovers hiding wrapped in shadows,
The city of people sitting and talking quietly
Beyond shut doors and walls as thick as a century,
People who laugh too little and too loudly,
Whose tears fall inward, flowing back to the heart.

I am the city whose fog will fall like a finger gently
Erasing the anger of angles, the strident indecorous gesture,
Whose dusk will come like tact, like a change in the conversation,
Violet and indigo, with strings of lemon street-lamps
Casting their pools into the pools of rain
As the notes of the piano are cast from the top-floor window
Into the square that is always Sunday afternoon.

A. S. J. Tessimond

City River Blues

Went to the river
Seeking inspiration,
Saw dead fish floating
Dead men boating
And condoms galore.

Sat by the river
Wondering,
From where cometh
Dat bloody smell,
For if I waz wize
And I could tell
The world would know.

This is our river
It runs through our lives
This is our river
Our shit-coloured river,
It's had it
But it's ours.

This river speaks
Every boot had a body
Every shirt had a friend,
And the old boys
Say they shall all meet
Where every river ends.

Here by this river
Joe Public wrote songs
And ships came
From far away,
Capitalism lived here,
Ships left from here,
To cheat someone,
Somewhere.

This river is on the map
The Queen came here,
The King came here,
Hitler bombed it,
Joe Bloggs bombed it,
A hundred factories
Bomb it every day,
But this river won't go away,
They say.

Went to the river
Seeking inspiration,
Got eco-depression,
Got stopped and searched,
Got called a coon,
Got damned lungs,
Got city river blues.

Benjamin Zephaniah

THE QUEUE

What could be more British than the queue? Surely no other nation forms an orderly line with such docility. To be caught queue-jumping is surely the most public humiliation that most of us will ever have to endure. Post Offices have some of the most tortuously slow-moving queues in Britain, here commemorated by Fleur Adcock.

Post Office

The queue's right out through the glass doors
to the street: Thursday, pension day.
They built this Post Office too small.
Of course, the previous one was smaller –
a tiny prefab, next to the betting-shop,
says the man who's just arrived;
and the present one, at which we're queuing,
was cherry trees in front of a church.
The church was where the supermaket is:
'My wife and I got married in that church,'
the man says. 'We hold hands sometimes
when we're standing waiting at the checkout –
have a little moment together!' He laughs.
The queue shuffles forward a step.
Three members of it silently vow
never to grow old in this suburb;
one vows never to grow old at all.
'I first met her over there,' the man says,
'on that corner where the bank is now.
The other corner was Williams Brothers –
remember Williams Brothers? They gave you tokens,
tin money, like, for your dividend.'

The woman in front of him remembers.
She nods, and swivels her loose lower denture,
remembering Williams Brothers' metal tokens,
and the marble slab on the cheese-counter,
and the carved mahogany booth where you went to pay.
The boy in front of her is chewing gum;
his jaws rotate with the same motion
as hers: to and fro, to and fro.

Fleur Adcock

On the Sidelines

Who are these – stooping and shuffling
like old men in black plastic macs
    in an endless bus queue
        on a rainy day?

The buses which splash by and never stop
have drivers with the face of tanker captains
    who threw the switch
        to flush the tank

to spill the slick which was the death
of these little old men of the sea:
    puffin, cormorant, shag,
        gull, gannet, guillemot . . .

Philip Gross

Early Bird Blues

I am the early bird.
I have worn out my shoes
Simply because I heard
First come was first to choose.
One of my talents is avoiding queues.

I never ask how long
I shall be made to wait.
I have done nothing wrong.
I don't exaggerate.
To state the obvious, I'm never late.

Why has the queue not grown?
Nobody hears me speak.
I stand here all alone
Which makes me look unique
But even so, the worm avoids my beak.

What do the others know?
Have I been told a lie?
Why don't I turn and go?
I still know how to fly,
But, damn, I want that worm. I don't know why.

Sophie Hannah

CHRISTMAS AND EASTER

Depending on your cast of mind, it is either a national strength or weakness that our state church is the subject of so much gentle derision. Personally I think it is a strength and so, clearly, did John Betjeman who, though a devout Anglican, saw no reason to refrain from teasing the church he loved. For matters of life and death, read 'Days' by Philip Larkin, a confirmed agnostic.

Diary of a Church Mouse

Here among long-discarded cassocks,
Damp stools, and half-split open hassocks,
Here where the Vicar never looks
I nibble through old service books.
Lean and alone I spend my days
Behind this Church of England baize.
I share my dark forgotten room
With two oil-lamps and half a broom.
The cleaner never bothers me,
So here I eat my frugal tea.
My bread is sawdust mixed with straw;
My jam is polish for the floor.

Christmas and Easter may be feasts
For congregations and for priests,
And so may Whitsun. All the same,
They do not fill my meagre frame.
For me the only feast at all
Is Autumn's Harvest Festival,
When I can satisfy my want
With ears of corn around the font.
I climb the eagle's brazen head
To burrow through a loaf of bread.
I scramble up the pulpit stair
And gnaw the marrows hanging there.

      It is enjoyable to taste
These items ere they go to waste,
But how annoying when one finds
That other mice with pagan minds
Come into church my food to share
Who have no proper business there.
Two field mice who have no desire
To be baptized, invade the choir.
A large and most unfriendly rat
Comes in to see what we are at.
He says he thinks there is no God
And yet he comes . . . It's rather odd.
This year he stole a sheaf of wheat
(It screened our special preacher's seat),
And prosperous mice from fields away
Come in to hear the organ play,
And under cover of its notes
Eat through the altar's sheaf of oats.
A Low Church mouse, who thinks that I
Am too papistical, and High,
Yet somehow doesn't think it wrong
To munch through Harvest Evensong,
While I, who starve the whole year through,
Must share my food with rodents who
Except at this time of the year
Not once inside the church appear.

Within the human world I know
Such goings-on could not be so,
For human beings only do
What their religion tells them to.
They read the Bible every day
And always, night and morning, pray,
And just like me, the good church mouse,
Worship each week in God's own house,
  But all the same it's strange to me
How very full the church can be
With people I don't see at all
Except at Harvest Festival.

Sir John Betjeman

In Church

'And now to God the Father,' he ends.
And his voice thrills up to the topmost tiles:
Each listener chokes as he bows and bends.
And emotion pervades the crowded aisles.
Then the preacher glides to the vestry-door.
And shuts it, and thinks he is seen no more.

The door swings softly ajar meanwhile.
And a pupil of his in the Bible class.
Who adores him as one without gloss or guile.
Sees her idol stand with a satisfied smile
And re-enact at the vestry-glass
Each pulpit gesture in deft dumb-show
That had moved the congregation so.

Thomas Hardy

Days

What are days for?
Days are where we live.
They come, they wake us
Time and time over.
They are to be happy in:
Where can we live but days?

Ah, solving that question
Brings the priest and the doctor
In their long coats
Running over the fields.

Philip Larkin

HIGH TIDE

The sea is a rich source of metaphor for British poets.
Seamus Heaney uses a rocky peninsula to search for moral
definition. Tennyson equates the ceaseless pounding of the
waves with the remorselessness of his grief, and Matthew
Arnold makes Dover Beach the backdrop for his loss of
faith. In 'Beeny Cliff', Thomas Hardy remembers his first
wife, Emma. Memory is a wonderful thing as their union
was famously unhappy. During their marriage, Hardy
would only have visited Beeny Cliff with Emma for the
purposes of throwing her off it!

The Peninsula

When you have nothing more to say, just drive
For a day all round the peninsula.
The sky is tall as over a runway,
The land without marks, so you will not arrive

But pass through, though always skirting landfall.
At dusk, horizons drink down sea and hill,
The ploughed field swallows the whitewashed gable
And you're in the dark again. Now recall

The glazed foreshore and silhouetted log,
That rock where breakers shredded into rags,
The leggy birds stilted on their own legs,
Islands riding themselves out into the fog,

And drive back home, still with nothing to say
Except that now you will uncode all landscapes
By this: things founded clean on their own shapes,
Water and ground in their extremity.

Seamus Heaney

Dover Beach

The sea is calm to-night,
The tide is full, the moon lies fair
Upon the Straits; – on the French coast, the light
Gleams, and is gone; the cliffs of England stand,
Glimmering and vast, out in the tranquil bay.
Come to the window, sweet is the night air!
Only, from the long line of spray
Where the ebb meets the moon-blanch'd sand,
Listen! you hear the grating roar
Of pebbles which the waves suck back, and fling,
At their return, up the high strand,
Begin, and cease, and then again begin,
With tremulous cadence slow, and bring
The eternal note of sadness in.

   Sophocles long ago
Heard it on the Aegaean, and it brought
Into his mind the turbid ebb and flow
Of human misery; we
Find also in the sound a thought,
Hearing it by this distant northern sea.

The sea of faith
Was once, too, at the full, and round earth's shore
Lay like the folds of a bright girdle furl'd;
But now I only hear
Its melancholy, long, withdrawing roar,
Retreating to the breath

Matthew Arnold

Beeny Cliff

O the opal and the sapphire of that wandering western sea,
And the woman riding high above with bright hair flapping free –
The woman whom I loved so, and who loyally loved me.

The pale mews plained below us, and the waves seemed far away
In a nether sky, engrossed in saying their ceaseless babbling say,
As we laughed light-heartedly aloft on that clear-sunned March
     day.

A little cloud then cloaked us, and there flew an irised rain,
And the Atlantic dyed its levels with a dull misfeatured stain,
And then the sun burst out again, and purples prinked the main.

– Still in all its chasmal beauty bulks old Beeny to the sky,
And shall she and I not go there once again now March is nigh,
And the sweet things said in that March say anew there by and by?

What if still in chasmal beauty looms that wild weird western shore,
The woman now is – elsewhere – whom the ambling pony bore,
And nor knows nor cares for Beeny, and will laugh there
     nevermore.

Thomas Hardy

Break, Break, Break

Break, break, break,
On thy cold gray stones, O Sea!
And I would that my tongue could utter
The thoughts that arise in me.

O well for the fisherman's boy,
That he shouts with his sister at play!
O well for the sailor lad,
That he sings in his boat on the bay!

And the stately ships go on
To their haven under the hill:
But O for the touch of a vanish'd hand,
And the sound of a voice that is still!

Break, break, break,
At the foot of thy crags, O Sea!
But the tender grace of a day that is dead
Will never come back to me.

Lord Alfred Tennyson

MAD DOGS AND ENGLISHMEN

I hope the other British nations won't feel insulted if the poems in this section concentrate on *English* bloody-mindedness. All the poems here are gently mocking of English stubborness / philistinism / xenophobia / misanthropy, but at the same time there is a hint of pride at the extent of English wrongheadedness. I really like Kit Wright's poem 'Everyone Hates the English' which makes fun of our national sport of putting ourselves down. I was delighted to come across 'Finders Keepers' by John Agard, which is the perfect retort to the famous Noel Coward lyric about mad dogs and Englishmen.

from *Mad Dogs and Englishmen*

Mad dogs and Englishmen
Go out in the midday sun,
The Japanese don't care to.
The Chinese wouldn't dare to,
Hindoos and Argentines sleep firmly from twelve to one.
But Englishmen detest a siesta.
In the Philippines
There are lovely screens
To protect you from the glare.
In the Malay States
There are hats like plates
Which the Britishers won't wear.
At twelve noon
The natives swoon
And no further work is done.
But mad dogs and Englishmen
Go out in the midday sun.

Noel Coward

Finders Keepers

This morning on the way to Charing Cross
I found a stiff upper lip
lying there on the train seat

Finders Keepers
I was tempted to scream

But something about that stiff upper lip
left me speechless

It looked so abandoned so unloved
like a frozen glove
nobody bothers to pick up

I could not bear to hand in
that stiff upper lip
to the Lost & Found

So I made a place for it
in the lining of my coat pocket

and I said
Come with me to the Third World

You go thaw off

John Agard

Mr Jones

'There's been an accident!' they said,
'Your servant's cut in half; he's dead!'
'Indeed!' said Mr Jones, 'and please
Send me the half that's got my keys.'

Harry Graham

Note on Intellectuals

To the man-in-the-street, who, I'm sorry to say
   Is a keen observer of life,
The word Intellectual suggests straight away
   A man who's untrue to his wife.

W. H. Auden

The World State

Oh, how I love Humanity,
    With love so pure and pringlish,
And how I hate the horrid French,
    Who never will be English!

The International Idea,
    The largest and the clearest,
Is welding all the nations now,
    Except the one that's nearest.

This compromise has long been known,
    This scheme of partial pardons,
In ethical societies
    And small suburban gardens –

The villas and the chapels where
    I learned with little labour
The way to love my fellow-man
    And hate my next-door neighbour.

G. K. Chesterton

I Wish I Loved the Human Race

I wish I loved the Human Race;
I wish I loved its silly face;
I wish I liked the way it walks;
I wish I liked the way it talks;
And when I'm introduced to one,
I wish I thought 'What Jolly Fun!'

Sir Walter Raleigh

The Bloody Orkneys

This bloody town's a bloody cuss
No bloody trains, no bloody bus,
And no one cares for bloody us
In bloody Orkney.

The bloody roads are bloody bad,
The bloody folks are bloody mad,
They'd make the brightest bloody sad,
In bloody Orkney.

All bloody clouds, and bloody rains,
No bloody kerbs, no bloody drains,
The Council's got no bloody brains,
In bloody Orkney.

Everything's so bloody dear,
A bloody bob, for bloody beer,
And is it good? – no bloody fear,
In bloody Orkney.

The bloody 'flicks' are bloody old,
The bloody seats are bloody cold,
You can't get in for bloody gold
In bloody Orkney.

The bloody dances make you smile,
The bloody band is bloody vile,
It only cramps your bloody style,
In bloody Orkney.

No bloody sport, no bloody games,
No bloody fun, the bloody dames
Won't even give their bloody names
In bloody Orkney.

Best bloody place is bloody bed,
With bloody ice on bloody head,
You might as well be bloody dead,
In bloody Orkney.

Captain Hamish Blair

Everyone Hates the English

Everyone hates the English,
   Including the English. They sneer
At each other for being so English,
   So what are they doing here,
The English? It's *thick* with the English,
   All over the country. Why?
Anyone ever born English
   Should shut up, or fuck off, or die.

Anyone ever born English
   Should hold their extraction in scorn
And apologise all over England
   For ever at all being born,
For that's how it is, being English;
   Fodder for any old scoff
That England might be a nice country
   If only the English fucked off!

Kit Wright

OOH, YOU ARE AWFUL!

I was going to call this section 'Oh, Matron' but I can't remember whether matrons exist anymore. But I felt I couldn't complete this anthology of poems about Britain today without at least a nod and wink to the great British tradition of smut and sauciness. From the Anglo-Saxon riddles through Chaucer to the Earl of Rochester and right up to our own dirty limericks and Roger McGough, we British can do bawdy with brio.

Anglo-Saxon Riddle 25

I am a strange creature, for I satisfy women . . .
a service to the neighbours. No one suffers
at my hands except for my slayer.
I grow very tall, erect in a bed,
I'm hairy underneath. From time to time
A beautiful girl, the brave daughter
Of some fellow dares to hold me
Grips my reddish skin, robs me of my head
And puts me in the pantry. At once that girl
With plaited hair who has confined me
Remembers our meeting. Her eye moistens.

Anonymous

Administration

Day by day your estimation clocks up
Who deserves a smile and who a frown.
And girls you have to tell to pull their socks up
And those whose pants you'd most like to pull down.

Philip Larkin

A Hand in the Bird

I am a maiden who is forty,
And a maiden I shall stay.
There are some who call me haughty,
But I care not what they say.

I was running the tombola
At our church bazaar today,
And doing it with gusto
In my usual jolly way . . .

When suddenly, I knew not why,
There came a funny feeling
Of something *crawling up my thigh*!
I nearly hit the ceiling!

A mouse! I thought. How foul! How mean!
How exquisitely tickly!
Quite soon I know I'm going to scream.
I've got to catch it quickly.

I made a grab. I caught the mouse,
Now right inside my knickers.
A mouse my foot! It was a HAND!
Great Scott! It was the vicar's!

Roald Dahl

The Ruined Maid

'O'Melia, my dear, this does everything crown!
Who could have supposed I should meet you in Town?
And whence such fair garments, such prosperi-ty?' –
'O didn't you know I'd been ruined?' said she.

'You left us in tatters, without shoes or socks,
Tired of digging potatoes, and spudding up docks;
And now you've gay bracelets and bright feathers three!' –
'Yes: that's how we dress when we're ruined,' said she.

'At home in the barton you said "thee" and "thou",
And "thik oon", and "theäs oon", and "t'other"; but now
Your talking quite fits 'ee for high compa-ny!' –
'Some polish is gained with one's ruin,' said she.

'Your hands were like paws then, your face blue and bleak
But now I'm bewitched by your delicate cheek,
And your little gloves fit as on any la-dy!' –
'We never do work when we're ruined,' said she.

'You used to call home-life a hag-ridden dream,
And you'd sigh, and you'd sock; but at present you seem
To know not of megrims or melancho-ly!' –
'True. One's pretty lively when ruined,' said she.

'I wish I had feathers, a fine sweeping gown,
And a delicate face, and could strut about Town!' –
'My dear – a raw country girl, such as you be,
Cannot quite expect that. You ain't ruined,' said she.

Thomas Hardy

The Young Lady of Exeter

There was a young lady of Exeter
So pretty that men craned their necks at her
      And one went so far
      As to wave from his car
The distinguishing mark of his sex at her.

Anonymous

I Sometimes Think

I sometimes think that I should like
To be the saddle of a bike.

Anonymous

Some People

Some people like sex more than others –
You seem to like it a lot.
There's nothing wrong with being innocent or high-minded
But I'm glad you're not.

Wendy Cope

The Young Fellow of King's

There was a young fellow of King's
Who cared not for whores and such things
    For his secret desire
    Was a boy in the choir
With a bum like a jelly on springs.

Anonymous

Rural Rides: The Tractor Driver

When the tractor driver's ride is bumpy
He grits his teeth and thinks of scrumpy,
And that Dorset wench with winsome dimples
Who lives in Weymouth and has big Bristols.

Robert Maitre

THE SECOND OLDEST PROFESSION

I don't know why there are so many nasty poems about
British journalists. Why anyone would want to malign such
a fine, upstanding group of men and women is beyond me.
But here is a very small selection to give you a flavour.
I can't imagine that any of my readers will agree with
these poems in any way.

Haiku: The Season of Celebrity

With summer comes the
bluebottle; with pleasant fame
comes the journalist.

Gavin Ewart

How to Deal with the Press

She'll urge you to confide. Resist.
Be careful, courteous, and cool.
Never trust a journalist.

'We're off the record,' she'll insist.
If you believe her, you're a fool.
She'll urge you to confide. Resist.

Should you tell her who you've kissed,
You'll see it all in print, and you ll
Never trust a journalist

Again. The words are hers to twist,
And yours the risk of ridicule.
She'll urge you to confide. Resist.

'But X is nice,' the publicist
Will tell you. 'We were friends at school.'
Never trust a journalist,

Hostile, friendly, sober, pissed,
Male or female – that's the rule.
When tempted to confide, resist.
Never trust a journalist.

Wendy Cope

The British Journalist

You cannot hope
to bribe or twist
(thank God!) the
British journalist.

But, seeing what
the man will do
unbribed, there's
no occasion to.

Humbert Wolfe

HOME THOUGHTS FROM ABROAD

It is invariably true that you don't know what you've got till it's gone. This is especially true of poets, who positively thrive on loss. Some of the finest, most evocative poems about Britain have been written by poets who have chosen quite voluntarily to live abroad. I love all the poems that follow: the intensity of their longing makes me look at my surroundings with new affection. However grim this country can be (see Kit Wright passim) I wouldn't want to live anywhere else.

Home thoughts, from Abroad

Oh, to be in England
Now that April's there,
And whoever wakes in England
Sees, some morning, unaware,
That the lowest boughs and the brushwood sheaf
Round the elm-tree bole are in tiny leaf,
While the chaffinch sings on the orchard bough
In England – now!
And after April, when May follows,
And the whitethroat builds, and all the swallows!
Hark, where my blossomed pear-tree in the hedge
Leans to the field and scatters on the clover
Blossoms and dewdrops – at the bent spray's edge –
That's the wise thrush; he sings each song twice over,
Lest you should think he never could recapture
The first fine careless rapture!
And though the fields look rough with hoary dew,
All will be gay when noontide wakes anew
The buttercups, the little children's dower
– Far brighter than this gaudy melon-flower!

Robert Browning

My Heart's in the Highlands

My heart's in the Highlands, my heart is not here;
My heart's in the Highlands a-chasing the deer;
Chasing the wild deer, and following the roe,
My heart's in the Highlands, wherever I go.
Farewell to the Highlands, farewell to the North,
The birth-place of valour, the country of worth;
Wherever I wander, wherever I rove,
The hills of the Highlands for ever I love.

Farewell to the mountains, high cover'd with snow;
Farewell to the straths and green valleys below;
Farewell to the forests and wild-hanging woods;
Farewell to the torrents and loud-pouring floods.
My heart's in the Highlands, my heart is not here;
My heart's in the Highlands a-chasing the deer;
Chasing the wild deer, and following the roe,
My heart's in the Highlands, wherever I go.

Robert Burns

from *The Old Vicarage, Grantchester*

Ah God! to see the branches stir
Across the moon at Grantchester!
To smell the thrilling-sweet and rotten
Unforgettable, unforgotten
River-smell, and hear the breeze
Sobbing in the little trees.
Say, do the elm-clumps greatly stand
Still guardians of that holy land?
The chestnuts shade, in reverend dream,
The yet unacademic stream?
Is dawn a secret shy and cold
Anadyomene, silver-gold?
And sunset still a golden sea
From Haslingfield to Madingley?
And after, ere the night is born,
Do hares come out about the corn?
Oh, is the water sweet and cool,
Gentle and brown, above the pool?
And laughs the immortal river still
Under the mill, under the mill?
Say, is there Beauty yet to find?
And Certainty? and Quiet kind?
Deep meadows yet, for to forget
The lies, and truths, and pain? . . . oh! yet
Stands the Church clock at ten to three?
And is there honey still for tea?

Rupert Brooke

'Into my heart an air that kills'

Into my heart an air that kills
   From yon far country blows:
What are those blue remembered hills,
   What spires, what farms are those?

That is the land of lost content,
   I see it shining plain,
The happy highways where I went
   And cannot come again.

A. E. Housman

from *In England*

The stone-built villages of England.
A cathedral bottled in a pub window.
Cows dispersed across the fields.
Monuments to kings.

A man in a moth-eaten suit
Sees a train off, heading, like everything here, for the sea,
Smiles at his daughter, leaving for the East.
A whistle blows.

And the endless sky over the tiles
Grows bluer as swelling birdsong fills.
And the clearer the song is heard,
The smaller the bird.

Joseph Brodsky

THE WAY WE LIVE NOW

The BBC recently invited its viewers to enter a competition to write a poem for Britain. The only rule was that the poem should be no more than sixteen lines and that the poem should not have been published before. The number and quality of the entries was extraordinary. Judging from the poems we received we are no longer a nation of shopkeepers but a nation of poets. The poems included here are truly representative of the wealth of poetic talent that Great Britain has to offer, and they all, in different ways, reflect on the way we live now.

Harvest Time: a Needlework Map commemorating the Millennium

Our village holds no special place
In history. Its public face
Would cause no traveller to pause,
Its landscape merits no applause.

We love it though. And love declares
Its memories, in patchwork squares,
And fabric images that bind
The heritage we leave behind.
Each public, private, thought portrayed,
Each delicately *appliquéd*.

We stretch our memories on frames,
Without exaggerated claims,
Knowing each proud biography
Embroiders our geography.
This warning, too, our needles know,
That as we reap, so shall we sew.

Con Connell

Earnestly Seeking

Distinguished, one-time colonial power,
Heart of oak, a naval soul,
Anchored uncertainly off Europe
Seeks harbour for similar role.

Mature, vibrant, stylish nation,
Still fun-loving, young at heart,
Seeks creative cultural identity,
Interested in pop and modern art.

Witty, enthusiastic, sport-loving,
Not just a hope and glory land,
Seeks warmer cosmopolitan image
To suit a wide-ranging national brand.

Considerate, sincere, yet confused country,
Values its past, yearns for applause,
Seeks genuine like-minded companions
For long-term friendship, possible common cause.

Maggie Ward

After all that

On Parents' Night, in the crumbling hall
of the Empire Street Infant and Junior School
a discomfort of strangers met to discuss
their children's future.
No one knew
exactly why the fight broke out, but suddenly

twelve Brummies, eleven Cockneys,
ten Taffies, nine Jocks, eight Micks,
seven Blacks, six Krauts,
five Scousers, four Frogs, three Pakis,
two Chinks and a Cornishwoman

were cussing one another across their children's heads

No-one knew exactly why it fizzled out
but all of a sudden someone said
I'd kill for a decent cup of tea.
Later, seventy eight mums and dads went home.

Ann Alexander

AUTHOR BIOGRAPHIES

FLEUR ADCOCK (1934–)
New Zealand poet and translator. Born in Papakura. Her family moved to England when she was five although returned after World War Two when she was thirteen. She returned to Britain in 1963 after she divorced fellow New Zealand poet, Alistair Campbell.

JOHN AGARD (1949–)
Playwright, poet, short-story and children's writer. Born in British Guyana, where he worked as a journalist before moving to England in 1977. He was appointed Writer in residence at the South Bank Centre in London, before becoming Poet in residence at the BBC. He won the Paul Hamlyn Award for poetry in 1997. His work includes *Man to Pan* (1982), winner of the Casa de las Américas Prize, *Limbo Dancer in Dark Glasses* (1983), *Mangoes and Bullets: Selected and New Poems 1972–84* (1985) and *Weblines* (2000).

MONIZA ALVI (1954–)
Poet. Born in Pakistan and grew up in Hertfordshire. After teaching at a secondary school she now works as a tutor for the Open College of the Arts. Her first collection *The Country at My Shoulder* (1993) was shortlisted for the T. S. Eliot and Whitbread poetry prizes. She was also co-winner of The Poetry Business Prize in 1991. Her other work includes *A Bowl of Warm Air* (1996) and *Souls* (2002).

SIMON ARMITAGE (1963–)
Poet, novelist and playwright. Born in Huddersfield. While working as a probation officer in Oldham, Manchester, his first collection *Zoom!* was published in 1989. His other poetry includes *Kid* (1992), *CloudCuckooLand* (1997), and *Selected Poems* (2001). He received the Lannan Literary Award for Poetry in 1994 and in 2002 was shortlisted for the T. S. Eliot Prize for *The Universal Home Doctor.*

MATTHEW ARNOLD (1822–1888)
British poet and critic. Born at Laleham-on-Thames, Surrey. Arnold's work included *Empedocles on Etna, and Other Poems* (1852), *Poems* (1853) and *Poems, Second Series* (1855). He was an inspector of schools between 1851 and 1883 He died of a heart attack on 15 April 1888 and was buried in the town where he was born.

PAM AYRES (1947–)
Poet. Born in Stanford-in-the-Vale, Berkshire. Her career as comic poet started when she first read her poetry on BBC Radio Oxford in 1974. She then appeared on ITV's *Opportunity*

Knocks in November 1975. Her most recent collection is *With These Hands* (1999) published by Weidenfeld & Nicolson.

SIR JOHN BETJEMAN (1906–1984)
British poet. Born in Highgate, London. Betjeman worked variously as a film critic for the *Evening Standard*, architectural critic and as a Press Officer in Dublin to the British representative. The IRA thought he was a spy and considered assassinating him. He suffered from Parkinson's disease later in life.

CAPTAIN HAMISH BLAIR (*aka* FRED MORGAN) (1921–)
The real identity of the author of this poem was not known until 1998 when Fred Morgan, a veteran of the Royal Navy, came across his own work in Solihull library, apparently unaware of the popularity of his verse. He wrote 'The Bloody Orkneys' in 1942 when he was based there for twelve months. Morgan claims that he actually liked the place but the other men based there were constantly moaning about the miserable weather and it was this that prompted him to write the poem. Morgan also explains one of the more obscure lines in the poem when he refers to it being impossible to get into cinemas '. . . for bloody gold': The 'gold' is not money but rather the gold-braided officers who generally took all the seats up in the cinema.

WILLIAM BLAKE (1757–1827)
British poet and artist. Born in London. He married an illiterate woman named Catherine Boucher in 1772, whom he taught to read and to write. His most popular collection, *Songs of Innocence*, appeared in 1789, followed by *Songs of Experience* (1794).

JOSEPH BRODSKY (1940–1996)
Poet and essayist. Born in Leningrad. He began writing when he was eighteen, and was recognised by poet Anna Akhmatova as one of the greatest lyric voices of his generation. His work includes *A Part of Speech* (1980), *Joseph Brodsky: Selected Poems* (1973), and *To Urania* (1988). He won the Nobel prize for literature in 1987.

RUPERT (CHAWNER) BROOKE (1887–1915)
English poet. Born Rugby, Warwickshire. Though known as a war poet, strictly speaking Brooke was a Georgian poet with a broad range of poetical subject matter – from imagining the world from a fish's point of view, through to the growing old disgracefully of 'Menelaus and Helen'. He died on a hospital ship off the island of Scyros during World War One of septicaemia resulting from a mosquito bite.

THOMAS EDWARD BROWN (1830–1897)
Born in Douglas, the Isle of Man. He spent much of his life teaching, holding positions at various schools in Britain. His work includes *Betsy Lee, The Doctor and Other Poems, The Manx Witch and Other Poems, The Collected Poems of T. E. Brown.*

ROBERT BROWNING (1812–1889)
British poet born in Camberwell, London. Married poet Elizabeth Barrett Browning with whom he had established a literary correspondence. They eloped in 1846 to escape her overbearing father. Browning wrote prolifically – *Sordello* and *The Ring and the Book* are among his many works. On the day of his death in December 1889, his last poems were published.

CHARLES CAUSLEY (1917–)
Playwright, poet and children's author. Born in Launceston, Cornwall. His work includes *Farewell, Aggie Weston* (1951), *Survivor's Leave* (1953), *Union Street: Poems* (1957) and *The Young Man of Cury and Other Poems* (1991). He was awarded the Queen's Gold Medal for Poetry in 1967. He has also won the Ingersoll/T. S. Eliot Award (1990). In 2000 he was awarded the Heywood Hill Literary Prize.

G. K. CHESTERTON (1874–1936)
English writer. Born in Beaconsfield. He started off working for two magazines, *The Bookman* and *The Speaker*, as a journalist. In 1902 he was given a regular weekly opinion column in the *Daily News* and in 1905 he started writing a column for the *Illustrated London News*. His work includes *The Man Who Was Thursday*, *Manalive*, *The Flying Inn*, *St Francis of Assisi*, *The Everlasting Man*, *Tales of the Long Bow* and *Chaucer and Thomas Aquinas* amongst others.

MANDY COE (1962–)
Born in London. Coe currently resides in Aigburth, Liverpool. She is a visual artist as well as a poet. She also runs writing workshops in schools and community centres. Her most recent collection is *Pinning the Tail on the Donkey* (2000).

WENDY COPE (1945–)
Poet, whose work includes *Making Cocoa for Kingsley Amis* (1986), and *Serious Concerns* (1992). Cope trained as a teacher and worked as a television columnist for *The Spectator* between 1986–1990.

NOEL (PIERCE) COWARD (1899–1973)
Playwright and poet. Born in Teddington he started a stage career as an actor at 12 and emerged as a talented playwright with *The Vortex* in 1924. Though Coward loved to satirise the high society and aristocratic circles of which he was a part, he also had a strong sense of national pride, expressed in lyrics such as 'Mad Dogs and Englishmen'. His most famous work includes plays such as *Hay Fever* and *Private Lives* amongst others.

WILLIAM COWPER (1731–1800)
British writer. Born in Berkhampstead, Hertfordshire. He suffered from depression in his earlier life – recovery from which coincided with his conversion to evangelical Christianity. His work includes the *Olney Hymns, John Gilpin* and *The Task*, as well as translations of Homer which he published in 1791.

TONY CURTIS (1946–)
Born in Carmarthen, Wales. He has published seventeen books of criticism, poetry and anthologies. His most recent work is *Heaven's Gate* (2001). He won an Eric Gregory Award in 1972, the National Poetry competition in 1984, the Dylan Thomas Award in 1993 and the Cholmondeley award for services to poetry from the Society of Authors in 1998. He is currently Professor of Poetry at the University of Glamorgan.

ROALD DAHL (1916–1990)
British writer. Born in Llanduff, South Wales, of Norwegian parents. Roald Dahl was one of the greatest story-tellers of all time. He was a fighter pilot for the RAF during World War Two and almost died after his plane crashed. His writing career started shortly after this near-death experience. His work includes *Tales of the Unexpected*, *James and the Giant Peach*, *The Witches* and *Charlie and the Chocolate Factory*.

JULIA DARLING (1956–)
British poet, novelist and short story writer. She worked as a community arts worker in Sunderland, England between 1980 and 1986 before becoming a full-time writer from 1988. Her work includes *Sauce* (1993), *Bloodlines* (1995) and *Crocodile Soup* (1998).

DES DILLON (1961–)
Poet, dramatist and screenwriter. Born in Coatbridge, Scotland. He studied English at Strathclyde University and subsequently taught English. He won the Television Arts Performance Showcase Writer of the Year award in 2000 and 2001. His work includes *Me and Ma Gal, The Big Empty, Duck, Itchycooblue, Return of the Busby Babes* and *The Big Q.*

GAVIN (BUCHANAN) EWART (1916–1996)
British poet. He first published poems at the age of 17. After serving in the Royal Artillery between 1940–1946 he worked for the British Council and then became an advertising copywriter until 1971. He subsequently became a full-time free-lance writer.

U. A. FANTHORPE (1929–)
Born in Kent. She was the first woman to be nominated for the post of Oxford Professor of Poetry. She was made CBE in 2001 for services to poetry and in 2003 received the Queen's Gold Medal for Poetry. For a time she worked as a hospital clerk in Bristol and the experience provided the backdrop to her first collection *Side Effects* (1978). Her other work includes *Consequences* (2000), *Christmas Poems* (2002), *Queuing for the Sun* (2003) and *New & Collected Poems 1978–2003* (2003).

JAMES FENTON (1949–)
Poet and reporter. Born in Durham. His work includes *Terminal Moraine* (1972), *The Memory of War* (1982), *Manila Envelope* (1989), *Partingtime Hall* (1987) written with John Fuller, and *Out of Danger* (1993). He has also worked as a political and literary journalist.

HENRY FIELDING (1707–1754)
English writer. Born at Wedmore,
England. His work includes *The
Modern Husband, Don Quixote in
England, An Apology for the Life of
Mrs Shamela Andrews, The History
of the Adventures of Joseph Andrews*
and *The History of Tom Jones, a
Foundling.*

HARRY (JOSCELYN CLIVE) GRAHAM
(1874–1936)
British Poet. He signed his poems
with the name Col. D. Streamer,
taken from the regiment to which he
belonged, the Coldstream Guards.
His best known collection is his
*Ruthless Rhymes for Heartless
Homes.*

HENRY GRAHAM (1930–)
Born in Liverpool. Lecturer in Art
History at Liverpool Polytechnic. His
work includes *Poker in Paradise Lose*
(1977), *Bomb* (1985), *Europe After
Rain* (1982), *The Very Fragrant Death
of Paul Gauguin* (1987), *Everywhere
You Look* (1993), *The Eye of the
Beholder* (1997), and *Bar Room
Ballads* (1999).

THOMAS GRAY (1716–1771)
British poet. Born in Cornhill,
London. He trained as a lawyer
before becoming an academic at
Cambridge. His work includes *Ode
on the Spring, The Fatal Sisters, A
Long Story, Elegy Written in a
Country Churchyard, Ode to
Adversity* and the poem included
here *Ode on the Death of a Favourite
Cat, Drowned in a Tub of Goldfishes* –
written in Augustan mock-epic
vogue.

SOPHIE HANNAH (1971–)
British poet and novelist. Born in
Manchester where she currently
teaches at Manchester Metropolitan
University's Writing School. Her
work includes *Gripless* (1999),
Cordial and Corrosive (2000) and
The Superpower of Love (2001). Her
poetry includes the Arts Council
award-winning *Hotels Like Houses*
(1996), and *Leaving and Leaving
You* (1999).

THOMAS HARDY (1840–1928)
Poet and novelist. Born in Dorset,
England. Hardy worked as an
architect in his early years. His first
novel, *Desperate Remedies,* was
published in 1871, and Hardy was
soon successful enough to leave
the field of architecture for writing.
His novels include *Tess of the
D'Urbervilles, Jude the Obscure,
Far From the Madding Crowd.* He
published eight collections of
poetry in his lifetime including
Wessex Poems, and *Satires of
Circumstance.*

TONY HARRISON (1937–)
Poet, translator, dramatist, and
librettist. Born in Leeds. His work
includes *Laureate's Block* (2000),
The Shadow of Hiroshima (1995),
The Gaze of the Gorgon (1992) –
which was awarded the Whitbread
Prize for Poetry – and *Selected
Poems* (1984).

SEAMUS HEANEY (1939–)
Irish poet. Born in Co. Derry,
Northern Ireland. He won the Nobel
Prize for literature in 1995. His
collections of poetry include *The*

Haw Lantern (1987), *New Selected Poems 1966–1987* (1990), *Seeing Things* (1991).

FELICIA DOROTHEA BROWNE HEMANS (1793–1835)
British poet. Born in Liverpool. A gifted child with a photographic memory, her first book of poems was published when she was fourteen. Her subsequent volumes of poetry were extremely popular and sold well enough to support her and her children. Her work includes *The Domestic Affections and Other Poems*, *The Restoration of the Works of Art to Italy*, *Translations from Camoens and Other Poems*. It was Hemans who wrote the poem *Casabianca* upon which Elizabeth Bishop based her famous poem of the same name.

GERARD MANLEY HOPKINS (1844–1889)
Poet. Born in Stratford, Essex. He converted to Catholicism in 1867 when he decided to burn all the poetry he had written to date and vowed to 'write no more . . . unless it were by the wish of my superiors'. The wreck of a German ship at the mouth of the Thames, the *Deutschland*, galvanised him into writing poetry again. Hopkins introduced in this poem the metrical method that he is still known for today – 'sprung rhythm'. His poems were all published posthumously by his friend Robert Bridges. He wrote prolifically and his work includes such memorable poems as 'Binsey Poplars', 'God's Grandeur' and of course 'Pied Beauty'.

THOMAS HOOD (1799–1845)
Poet. Born in London. He worked variously as a clerk and an engraver before assuming various editorial positions on literary magazines. He is known chiefly as a humourist for poems such as *Odes and Addresses to Great People* and *Whims and Oddities*.

A. E. HOUSMAN (1859–1936)
British poet and scholar. Born in Fockbury, England. The collection for which Housman is best known, *A Shropshire Lad*, was published in 1896 at his own expense.

JACKIE KAY (1961–)
British poet, playwright, and novelist. Born in Edinburgh, Scotland. Her mother was Scottish and her father was Nigerian. She was adopted by a white couple and brought up in Glasgow. Her work includes *Other Lovers* (1993), *Twice Through the Heart* (1997), *Trumpet* (1998), *Off Colour* (1998) and *Why Don't You Stop Talking* (2002).

JOHN KEATS (1795–1821)
British Romantic poet. After his schooling Keats trained as a surgeon. In 1814 he sacrificed his ambition to be a doctor to devote himself to literature. His most famous poems include 'Endymion', 'Ode to a Nightingale', 'The Eve of St Agnes', 'Ode to Melancholy' and 'Ode to Autumn'. Keats died aged twenty-six of tuberculosis.

RUDYARD KIPLING (1865–1936)
Poet and novelist. Born in Bombay, but educated in England at the United Services College, Westward Ho, Bideford. He is the quintessential poet of the British Empire. His work includes *Barrack Room Ballads*, *Jungle Book*, *Stalky and Co.*, *Just So Stories*, *Kim*, *Puck of Pook's Hill*, *Debits and Credits* and the *The Second Jungle Book*. He received the Gold Medal of the Royal Society of Literature in 1926 which only Walter Scott, George Meredith, and Thomas Hardy had been awarded before him.

B. C. (BARRY CAVENDISH) LEALE (1930–)
British poet. Born in Ashford, Middlesex. As well as writing poetry Leale has also worked variously as a bookseller and sales assistant. His work includes *Under a Glass Sky*, *Preludes*, and *The Poetry Book Society Anthology 1986–87*.

PHILIP LARKIN (1922–85)
British poet. Born in Coventry. Larkin worked as a librarian variously at the University of Leicester and Queen's University, Belfast. He was a great jazz aficionado and reviewed for the *Daily Telegraph*.

LACHLAN MACKINNON (1956–)
Scottish poet. Born in Aberdeen. He has reviewed for the *Times Literary Supplement*, the *Independent*, the *Daily Telegraph*, the *Guardian*, the *Observer* and *Poetry Review*. He received an Eric Gregory Award in 1985. He has published three volumes

of poetry, *Monterey Cypress* (1988), *The Coast of Bohemia* (1991) and *The Jupiter Collisions* (2003).

ANDREW MARVELL (1621–78)
British metaphysical poet. Marvell was born in Winestead-in-Holderness in 1621. His work included 'Upon Appleton House', 'The Garden', and his most famous poem 'To his Coy Mistress'.

GLYN MAXWELL (1962–)
British poet, novelist and playwright. Born in Welwyn Garden City. His work includes *Time's Fool* (2000), *Rest for the Wicked* (1995), and *The Breakage* (1999). In 1997 the American Academy of Arts and Letters awarded him the E. M. Forster Prize.

ROGER MCGOUGH (1937–)
British poet. His work includes *Watchword* (1969), *Gig* (1972), *Waving at Trains* (1982), *The Stowaways* (1986), *An Imaginary Menagerie* (1988), and *Eclipse* (2002).

A. A. (ALAN ALEXANDER) MILNE (1882–1956)
Playwright, essayist, novelist and poet. Born in London. Worked as an assistant editor for *Punch* in the years leading up to the First World War, when he enlisted in the Royal Warwickshire Regiment. He wrote his first play *Wurzel-Flummery* in 1917. The birth of his son Christopher Robin Milne inspired him to write the verse for which he is so famous, writing his first collection *When We Were Very Young* in 1924, followed

up with *Winnie-the-Pooh*, *The House at Pooh Corner*, and *Now We Are Six*.

SIR WALTER RALEIGH (1554–1618)
Soldier, explorer, courtier and writer. Born at Hayes Barton, Devon, England. He was, for a time, a court favourite of Queen Elizabeth I – as such he was granted a wine monopoly, given estates in Ireland and appointed captain of the Queen's guard. His work includes 'In Commendation of The Steel Glass', 'The Excuse', 'An Epitaph Upon the Right Honourable Philip Sidney', and his never completed *The History of the World*.

SYLVIA PLATH (1932–1963)
American poet born in Jamaica Plain, Massachusetts, Plath published her first poem when she was eight. She moved to Britain in 1959 with her husband of three years, Ted Hughes. Her work includes *The Colossus* (1960), *Ariel* (1965), *Crossing the Water* (1971), *Winter Trees* (1981) and her autobiographical book *The Bell-Jar* published in 1963 – the year she committed suicide.

TABITHA POTTS (1970–)
Writer. Born in Poole, Dorset. Had her first poem published age seven. After receiving a first in English language and literature at Oxford she has worked variously as a journalist, TV script editor and radio-producer. She currently lives in Spain with her husband Jason and son Felix. The title of the poem in this collection, *Dunravin'* was actually proposed by the author's partner, Jason Harman, as a name for their retirement home.

ANDREW SALKEY (1928–1995)
Novelist and poet. Born in Colon, Panama, of Jamaican parents. He worked for a brief spell at the BBC before he started teaching writing at Hampshire College, Amherst, Massachusetts. His work includes *Jamaica Symphony*, for which he received the Thomas Holmes Poetry Prize, and *A Quality of Violence*, which won him the Guggenheim fellowship. He received the Casa de Las Américas Poetry Prize for his *In the Hills Where Her Dreams Lie: Poems for Children*.

VERNON SCANNELL (1922–)
Scannell joined the army at the age of 18, fought and was wounded during World War Two. He deserted when the war with the Germans was finished because, in his words 'The Far East was not my concern'. He has led a varied and diverse life, earning a living as a boxer and tutor amongst other things. His work includes his autobiography *The Tiger and the Rose* (1983), *Collected Poems 1950–93* (1994), *Drums of Morning* (1999), and *Of Love and War* (2002).

SIR WALTER SCOTT (1771–1832)
Scottish poet and novelist. Born in Edinburgh. His work includes novels such as *Waverley*, *Rob Roy*, *The Heart of Midlothian* (1818), *The Bride of Lammermoor* (1819), and *The Legend of Montrose* (1819). However his passion for Scotland can be felt most strongly in his poetry. His poetic work includes *Minstrelsy of the Scottish Borders*, *The Lay of the Last Marmion* and *The Lady in the Lake*.

WILLIAM SHAKESPEARE
(1564–1616)
English poet and playwright born in
Henley Street in Stratford-upon-
Avon. He married Anne Hathaway
and had three children, Susanna,
Hamnet and Judith – though
Hamnet died tragically age eleven.
His plays include *King Lear*, *Hamlet*,
and *Romeo and Juliet*, amongst
numerous others. He is also famed
for his sonnet sequence, which
includes meditations on his own
fame and mortality.

CHRISTOPHER SMART (1722–1771)
British poet. Born in Shipbourne,
Kent, England. He published his first
collection of poetry in 1752, *Poems on
Several Occasions*. He also developed
a religious mania in 1750 which
meant that, in the words of his friend
Samuel Johnson, he was always
'falling upon his knees, and saying
his prayers in the street, or in any
other unusual place'. His best known
work includes *A Song to David*, and
Jubilate Agno from which 'My Cat
Jeoffrey' is taken.

(FLORENCE MARGARET) STEVIE
SMITH (1902–1971)
British writer. Born in Yorkshire. She
started her adult life as a secretary
with the magazine publisher George
Newnes and went on to be the
private secretary to Sir Nevill Pearson
and Sir Frank Newnes. She started
writing poetry in her twenties whilst
working at George Newnes. Her
work includes *Not Waving But
Drowning* (1957), *Selected Poems*
(1962), *The Frog Prince and Other
Poems* (1966), *The Best Beast* (1969),

Two in One (1971), *Scorpion and
Other Poems* (1972) and *Collected
Poems* (1975).

SYDNEY SMITH (1771–1845)
English clergyman, writer, and wit.
Born in Woodford, Essex. He was a
well-known figure in literary society.
His selected work was collected in
*The Selected Writings of Sydney
Smith*; edited, with an introduction
by W. H. Auden, published by
Farrar, Straus & Cudahy, 1956.

ALFRED LORD TENNYSON
(1809 1892)
Poet. Born in Somersby,
Lincolnshire. His success of his
Poems published in 1842 made
Tennyson a household name. In 1845
he received a government pension
of £200 a year, which helped relieve
his financial difficulties. It was the
success of *In Memoriam* and his
appointment as Poet Laureate in
1850 that sealed his reputation as
the most popular poet of the
Victorian era.

A. S. J. (ARTHUR SEYMOUR JOHN)
TESSIMOND (1902–1962)
Tessimond was born in Birkenhead.
He published three volumes of
poetry during his life. He worked in
bookshops and then as an advertising
copywriter.

EDWARD (PHILIP) THOMAS
(1878–1917)
English poet and journalist. Born in
Lambeth, London. Thomas started
writing poetry in 1912 under the
pseudonym Edward Eastaway, but a
meeting with the poet Robert Frost

in 1913 inspired him to concentrate
more fully on his poems.

R. S. (RONALD STUART) THOMAS
(1913–2000)
Welsh poet. Born in Cardiff in 1913.
He received his theological training
in Cardiff before becoming ordained
in 1936 and holding various curacies.
He married the painter Mildred E.
Eldridge whose death is the subject
of 'A Marriage'. The poem appears
in his *A Mass for Hard Times*
(1993).

STEVE TURNER (1949–)
Poet and writer. His first poem was
published in 1968. He has written
children's poetry as well as several
collections for adults, including
Poems (Lion Publishing 2002).

HUGO WILLIAMS (1942–)
British poet. Born in Windsor. Son
of actor Hugh Williams. He
published his first volume of poetry,
Symptoms of Loss, in 1965. His latest
work includes *Dock Leaves* (1994)
and *Billy's Rain* (1999).

JOHN WILMOT, SECOND EARL OF
ROCHESTER (1647–1680)
British poet. Born in Oxfordshire.
Rochester was famed for his
debauchery, as Samuel Johnson put
it 'he lived worthless and useless, and
blazed out his youth and health in
lavish voluptuousness'. He was
banished from court for an obscene
poem he wrote on Charles II.

HUMBERT WOLFE (1885–1940)
Poet. Born in Milan, Italy, his family
moved to Bradford when he was a

child. He started publishing poetry in
the 1920s. After the death of Robert
Bridges, he was in the running to
become the next Poet Laureate. As
well as his humorous verse such as
the quatrain on the British journalist,
he wrote more serious verse – the
most notable of which, *Requiem*
(1916), was published to great critical
acclaim.

WILLIAM WORDSWORTH
(1770–1850)
British poet. Born in Cockermouth,
Cumberland. In 1843 he succeeded
his friend Southey to the office of
Poet Laureate. His work includes
Poems in Two Volumes (1807) and
Lyrical Ballads (1798), whose second
edition featured a preface that
became a manifesto of the Romantic
movement.

KIT WRIGHT (1944–)
British writer and humourist.
His work includes *Hot Dog* (1982)
and *Cat Among the Pigeons* (1989),
and *Hoping It Might Be So: Poems
1974–2000* (2000). He has won the
Geoffrey Faber Memorial Prize, the
Poetry Society's Alice Hunt Bartlett
Prize, and the Hawthornden Prize
and was joint winner of the Royal
Society of Literature Heinemann
Award for his collection *Short
Afternoons* (1989).

BENJAMIN (OBADIAH IQBAL) ZEPHANIAH (1958–)

Born in Black River, Jamaica and moved to Birmingham at the age of two. His feelings about Britain are ambivalent, as he said in an interview with the *Observer* 'I gotta say I love this country, though I rail against it all the time. We all wanted a one-way ticket to Africa, but when I got there, I couldn't wait to get back'. His work includes *City Psalms* (1992), *Propa Propaganda* (1996), and *Too Black, Too Strong* (2001).

ACKNOWLEDGEMENTS

FLEUR ADCOCK: 'Post Office' from *Poems: 1960–2000* (Bloodaxe Books, 2000), reprinted by permission of the publishers. JOHN AGARD: 'My Brollie' from *Weblines* (Bloodaxe Books, 2000), reprinted by permission of the publishers, and 'Finders Keepers' from *Mangoes and Bullets: Selected and New Poems* (Pluto Press, 1985), reprinted by permission of the Caroline Sheldon Literary Agency on behalf of the author. MONIZA ALVI: 'Arrival 1946' from *Carrying My Wife* (Bloodaxe Books, 2000), reprinted by permission of the publishers. SIMON ARMITAGE: 'The Catch' from *Kid* (1992), reprinted by permission of the publishers, Faber & Faber, Ltd. W. H. AUDEN: 'Note on Intellectuals' from *W. H. Auden: The Collected Poems* (1976), reprinted by permission of the publishers, Faber & Faber, Ltd. PAM AYRES: 'Oh, I Wish I'd Looked After Me Teeth' from *The Works* (BBC Books, 1992), copyright © Pam Ayres 1992, reprinted by permission of Sheil Land Associates Ltd. HILAIRE BELLOC: 'Lord Finchley', 'The Justice of the Peace', and 'Henry King, Who Chewed String and was Cut Off Early in Dreadful Agonies' from *Complete Verse* (Duckworth, 1970), copyright © 1970 by the Estate of Hilaire Belloc, reprinted by permission of PFD on behalf of the Estate of Hilaire Belloc. JOHN BETJEMAN: 'Diary of a Church Mouse', 'In a Bath Teashop', 'Seaside Golf' and 'How to Get On in Society', from *Collected Poems* (1978), reprinted by permission of John Murray (Publishers) Ltd. CAPTAIN HAMISH BLAIR (alias Fred Morgan): 'The Bloody Orkneys'; copyright holder not traced. JOSEPH BRODSKY: 'From In England' from *Collected Poems in English* edited by Ann Kjellberg (2001), reprinted by permission of the publishers, Carcanet Press Ltd. ROBERT BROUGH: 'I'm A Shrimp!' first published in Punch; copyright holder not traced. CHARLES CAUSLEY: 'Timothy Winters' from *Collected Poems* (Macmillan, 1992), reprinted by permission of David Higham Associates. G. K. CHESTERTON: 'The Rolling English Road' and 'The World State' from *The Collected Poems of G. K. Chesterton* (Methuen, 1933), reprinted by permission of A. P. Watt Ltd on behalf of The Royal Literary Fund. WENDY COPE: 'English Weather' from *Serious Concerns* (1992), 'How to Deal with the Press' from *If I Don't Know* (2001), and 'From June to December V: Some People' from *Making Cocoa for Kingsley Amis* (1986), all reprinted by permission of the publishers, Faber & Faber Ltd. NOËL COWARD: lines from 'Mad Dogs and Englishmen from *Collected Verse* (Methuen 1984), copyright © The Estate of Noël Coward, reprinted by permission of Methuen Publishing Ltd. TONY CURTIS: 'Preparations' from *Selected Poems* (Poetry Wales Press, 1986), reprinted by permission of Seren Books. JULIA DARLING: 'Men on Trains', copyright © Julia Darling 1994, from *Sauce* by the Poetry Virgins (Bloodaxe/Diamond Twig, 1994), reprinted by permission of Curtis Brown, Ltd, London. ROALD DAHL: 'A Hand in the Bird' from

Rhyme Stew (Jonathan Cape, 1989), reprinted by permission of David Higham Associates Ltd. **DES DILLON**: 'Rain' from *Picking Brambles and Other Poems* (Luath Press, Edinburgh, 2003), reprinted by permission of the publisher. **GAVIN EWART**: 'On Proposed Legislation to Prevent British Woimen Importing Foreign Husbands' and 'Haiku: The Season of Celebrity' from *Collected Poems 1980–1990* (Hutchinson, 1991), reprinted by permission of Margo Ewart. **U. A. FANTHORPE**: 'Atlas' from *Safe As Houses* (Peterloo Poets, 1995), copyright © U. A. Fanthorpe 1995, reprinted by permission of the publishers. **HARRY GRAHAM**: 'Mr Jones' from *When Grandmama fell Off the Boat: The Best of Harry Graham* (Methuen, 1986), reprinted by permission of Laura Dance. **HENRY GRAHAM**: 'Not Cricket' from *Bar Room Ballads* (Ambit Books, 1999), reprinted by permission of the publishers. **PHILIP GROSS**: 'On the Sidelines' from *The All Nite Café* (1993), reprinted by permission of the publishers, Faber & Faber Ltd. **SOPHIE HANNAH**: 'Royal Wedding Poem' from *First of the Last Chances* (2003), 'Something Coming' and 'Early Bird Blues' from *The Hero and the Girl Next Door* (1995), reprinted by permission of the publishers, Carcanet Press Ltd. **TONY HARRISON**: 'National Trust' from *Selected Poems* (Penguin, 1987), reprinted by permission of Gordon Dickerson. **SEAMUS HEANEY**: 'Glanmore Sonnets' from *Field Work* (1979) and 'The Peninsula' from *Door into the Dark* (1969), reprinted by permission of the publishers, Faber & Faber Ltd. **A. E. HOUSMAN**: poems II ('Loveliest of trees') and XL ('Into my heart an air') from *The Shropshire Lad*, reprinted by permission of The Society of Authors as the Literary Representative of the Estate of A. E. Houseman. **JACKIE KAY**: 'In My Country' from *Other Lovers* (Bloodaxe Books, 1993) and 'Crown and Country' from *Off Colour* (Bloodaxe Books, 1998), reprinted by permission of the publishers. **RUDYARD KIPLING**: 'If–', 'The Way Through the Woods' and 'Four-Feet' from *Rudyard Kipling's Verse: The Definitive Edition* (Hodder & Stoughton, 1945), reprinted by permission of A. P. Watt Ltd on behalf of The National Trust for Places of Historic Interest or Natural Beauty. **PHILIP LARKIN**: 'An Arundel Tomb' from *Whitsun Weddings* (1964), 'Days', and 'Administration', from *Collected Poems* (1988) all reprinted by permission of the publishers, Faber & Faber Ltd: 'I Remember, I Remember' from *The Less Deceived* (Marvell Press, 1955), reprinted by permission The Marvell Press, London and Australia. **B. C. LEALE**: 'A Vegetation to be read by the Parsnip' from *Leviathan: and other Poems* (Allison & Busby, 1984), copyright © B. C. Leale 1984, reprinted by permission of the author. **ROGER MCGOUGH**: '40-Love' from *After the Merrymaking* (Jonathan Cape, 1971), copyright © Roger McGough 1971, reprinted by permission of PFD on behalf of the author. **LACHLAN MACKINNON**: 'Oxford' from *The Jupiter Collisions* (2003), reprinted by permission of the publishers, Faber & Faber Ltd. **ROBERT MAITRE**: 'Rural Rides: The Tractor Driver'; copyright holder not traced. **GLYN MAXWELL**: 'The Perfect Match' from *Out of the Rain* (Bloodaxe Books, 1992), reprinted by permission of Antony Harwood Ltd. **SPIKE MILLIGAN**: 'Teeth' from *Silly Verse for Kids* (Puffin, 1968) and 'A Have-It-Away Day' from *Hidden Words: Collected Poems* (Michael Joseph, 1995), reprinted by permission of Spike Milligan Productions Ltd. **A. A. MILNE**: 'Buckingham Palace' from *When We Were Very Young* (1924), reprinted by permission of the publishers, Egmont Books

Ltd, London. **TOM PAULIN**: 'The Civil Lovers' from *The Strange Museum* (1980), reprinted by permission of the publishers, Faber & Faber Ltd. **SYLVIA PLATH**: 'Blackberrying' from *Collected Poems* edited by Ted Hughes (1981), reprinted by permission of the publishers, Faber & Faber Ltd. **TABITHA POTTS**: 'Dunravin', copyright © Tabitha Potts 2003, first published in this collection, reprinted by permission of the author. **ANDREW SALKEY**: 'A Song for England' first published in *Caribbean Voices: Book 2* edited by John Figueroa (Evans, 1970), reprinted by permission of Patricia Salkey. **VERNON SCANNELL**: 'Burying Moses' from *The Best of Vernon Scannell* (Macmillan Children's Books, 2001), copyright © Vernon Scannell 2001, reprinted by permission of the author. **STEVIE SMITH**: 'The Englishwoman' and 'Happy Dogs of England' from *The Collected Poems of Stevie Smith* (Penguin Modern Classics, 1985), reprinted by permission of the Executors of James McGibbon. **A. S. J. TESSIMOND**: 'London' from *Voices in the City* (Heinemann, 1947), reprinted by permission of Sadie Williams. **STEVE TURNER**: 'British Rail Regrets', copyright © Steve Turner from *Poems* (Lion Publishing, 2002), reprinted by permission of the author and the publisher. **HUGO WILLIAMS**: 'Toilet' from *Collected Poems* (2002), reprinted by permission of the publishers, Faber & Faber Ltd. **HUMBERT WOLFE**: 'The British Journalist' from the verse novel *The Uncelestial City* (Victor Gollancz, 1930), copyright © Humbert Wolfe 1930, reprinted by permission of PFD on behalf of the Estate of Humbert Wolfe. **KIT WRIGHT**: 'Cricket Widow', 'Waiting for the 242', and 'Everyone Hates the English' from *Hoping It Might Be So* (Leviathan, 2000), reprinted by permission of the author. **BENJAMIN ZEPHANIAH**: 'City River Blues' from *Propa Propaganda* (Bloodaxe Books, 1996), reprinted by permission of the publishers.

The following poems are entries to a competition to find a Poem for Britain in the new millennium and are published here for the first time by permission of the authors: **CON CONNELL**: 'Harvest Time: A Needlework Map Commemorating the Millennium', copyright © Con Connell 2003; **MAGGIE WARD**: 'Earnestly Seeking', copyright © Maggie Ward 2003; **ANN ALEXANDER**: 'After All That', copyright © Ann Alexander 2003.

Although we have tried to trace and contact all copyright holders before publication, this has not been possible in every case. If notified, the publisher will be pleased to make any necessary arrangements at the earliest opportunity.

Thanks to Vanessa Lee, Rashna Nekoo and Kris Morris for all their help and support. Thanks also to Connie Hallam, copyright expert and Anne Jowett at the *Radio Times* for putting up with so much late copy, ditto to Kate Hyde and Michael Fishwick at HarperCollins. Undying gratitude to all at Talkback Thames especially Peter Fincham for allowing me such liberal use of the photocopier, and to Sally George, Alannah Richardson and all the *Essential Poems* team.

INDEX